# Healthy Screens, Happy Kids

## Practical Strategies for Raising Balanced Digital Natives

Navigate the digital age with confidence and connection.

**Ed Merid**

## Table of Contents

# Prologue: The Digital Crossroads

As I sit in my office, watching a mother struggle to pry a tablet from her crying toddler's hands. I am reminded of a similar scene from twenty years ago, except it was a parent trying to turn off the television before dinner. The more things change, the more they stay the same, yet today's digital landscape presents challenges our parents never imagined.

In my three decades of working with families, I've witnessed the transformation of childhood through the emergence of smartphones, tablets, social media, and AI-powered devices. I've seen the panic in parents' eyes as they ask, "Am I doing this right?" and heard the frustration in their voices when describing bedtime battles over screen time. I've also observed children flourishing with technology, creating remarkable digital art, coding their own games, and connecting with peers across continents.

This isn't a book about demonizing screens or promoting a tech-free childhood, such an approach would be both unrealistic and unhelpful in today's world. Instead, this is a guide for the modern parent standing at a digital crossroads, seeking balance in an increasingly connected world.

Think of technology as a powerful river flowing through our lives. We can't stop its flow, nor should we try. Our role as parents isn't to build a dam, but to teach our children to swim, to help them navigate these digital waters with confidence, purpose, and safety. Some days, you'll feel like you're floating seamlessly; other days, you might be paddling upstream. Both experiences are normal and part of the journey.

Drawing from the latest research in child development, neuroscience, and digital wellness, combined with real-world experiences from thousands of families I've counseled, this book offers practical strategies for creating a healthy digital environment in your home. You'll find evidence-based approaches, not quick fixes or rigid rules. Every family is unique, and what works for one may not work for another.

As you turn these pages, remember: you're not alone in this journey. Every parent today is part of the first generation raising children in a fully digital world. We're all learning as we go, adapting our approaches as technology evolves and our children grow.

My hope is that this book becomes your trusted companion in navigating the digital age with confidence, helping you raise children who don't just survive in the digital world but thrive in it. Children who use technology as a tool for growth, creativity, and connection while maintaining their well-being, relationships, and sense of self.

Let's begin this journey together, one screen at a time.

---

# Introduction: Welcome to the Digital Parenting Journey

Picture this: I'm sitting in my garden, watching my neighbor's kids. Seven-year-old Emma is teaching her grandfather how to use a tablet. Her teenage brother Jack is creating a family video blog with impressive editing skills. Meanwhile, their four-year-old sister Maya is melting down because her screen time is up. Sound familiar?

As a pediatric behavioral specialist and parent educator for over 10 years, I've seen countless moments like these. Each one reminds me how profoundly technology has transformed parenting. When I wrote my first book in 1998, our biggest worry was too much TV. Now?

I chuckle at how quaint that seems.

You're holding this book because, like millions of parents worldwide, you want answers.

Maybe you're wrestling with daily screen-time battles, worried about your teenager's endless scrolling, or debating whether your toddler should even touch an iPad. Take a deep breath. You've come to the right place.

### Why Balance Matters

Let me share a story that changed my perspective forever. In 2019, I met two families. The Thompsons banned screens entirely, leading to rebellion and secrecy among their teenagers. The Patels embraced technology with boundaries, fostering creativity and responsibility in their children.

That contrast taught me something crucial: our job isn't to fight technology. It's to teach our kids to balance on this digital tightrope; like learning to ride a bike. You don't stop falls by keeping them off bikes forever; you teach balance, braking, and navigation.

Here's what we know:

- Your children will inherit a world where digital literacy is as essential as reading.
- Technology can be a tool for growth; or a source of harm, depending on how it's used.
- Healthy digital habits, like table manners or road safety, don't happen by chance.

Through years of working with families, I've developed practical, adaptable strategies for real parents with real kids. This book isn't about perfection. It's about finding your family's digital balance.

In the chapters ahead, we'll explore how to:

- Make informed screen-time choices for every developmental stage.
- Turn passive screen time into active, meaningful engagement.
- Set boundaries that stick without constant battles.
- Recognize warning signs and respond effectively.
- Build lifelong habits for digital wellness.

You're not just managing screens. You're preparing your child for a digital future. Along the way, I'll share my own stories; my wins, my mistakes, and the lessons I've learned as both a professional and a parent.

So, let's turn the page and start this adventure together. Raising happy, healthy kids in the digital age doesn't mean being a perfect parent; it means being a present, informed, and adaptable one.

# Chapter 1: Understanding Screen Time

Let's get one thing straight: screen time is no longer a simple conversation. We're talking about something that's a fundamental part of our daily lives, reshaping the way our kids learn, communicate, and play. And with it comes a huge question: **How much is too much?**

It's not just about the hours they spend on devices, it's about "**what**" they're doing, "**how**" they're engaging, and "**when**" they're tuning in. Understanding the impact of screen time isn't as straightforward as it sounds, especially when different age groups react differently to technology. For some, it's a tool for learning. For others, it's a vortex that sucks them in for hours.

In this chapter, we'll unpack the science behind screen time, separating the myths from the facts. We'll explore the difference between passive and active screen use and discuss how screens impact brain development at various stages of childhood. It's important to know that not all screen time is created equal. What may seem harmless, like a child watching a cartoon, might actually be hindering their ability to focus, sleep, or socialize. And while some may think the best way to handle screen time is to shut it all down, we'll dive deeper into the real issue: balance.

This isn't about creating strict rules that don't fit with your family's lifestyle. It's about understanding what your child needs, how technology fits into that equation, and how to adjust your approach as your child grows.

By the end of this chapter, you'll have a clearer understanding of how screen time affects kids at different stages and how you can make informed choices to support your child's well-being while navigating the digital world.

## 1.1 : The Science of Screen Time

Screen time isn't just about passing the time or keeping kids entertained, there's a complex web of biological reactions that occurs when a child interacts with a screen. From how their brain processes information to the ways their body responds, the effects of screen time are far-reaching. Understanding these physiological and psychological responses is crucial for parents navigating this digital landscape. So, let's break it down and see what happens behind the scenes when kids engage with their devices.

**Dopamine Triggers: The Digital Reward System**

One of the first things to understand about screen time is its impact on dopamine, the brain's "feel-good" chemical. Every time a child interacts with their device, whether they're playing a video game, watching a YouTube video, or scrolling through social media, their brain releases dopamine. This neurotransmitter is associated with pleasure, motivation, and learning. Essentially, the brain is being "rewarded" every time it gets a digital hit.

For example, a child might feel a rush of excitement when they win a level in a game or when a new video pops up on their feed. At this moment, they're getting that dopamine rush, which feels rewarding, but it also encourages them to keep going. This can create a feedback loop where the brain craves more stimulation, leading to longer screen sessions and, at times, difficulty stopping. It's like an invisible hand that keeps pulling them back for more.

Research has shown that the rapid changes in screen content, flashes of colors, quick transitions, and immediate rewards, can overstimulate the brain, especially in children. Their dopamine receptors are still developing, meaning the brain's reward system reacts more intensely to these digital triggers. While a short burst of dopamine is natural and even necessary for motivation, when these triggers are too frequent or too intense, the brain can become desensitized. Over time, this could potentially lead to an over-reliance on digital rewards and make it harder for kids to engage in activities that don't offer instant gratification.

**Sleep Disruption: The Silent Culprit**

Next, let's address one of the most common and under-discussed effects of screen time: its impact on sleep. Most parents are familiar with the battle over screen time before bed, but the science behind why screens interfere with sleep is even more eye-opening.

When kids spend time in front of a screen, whether it's watching TV, playing games, or even reading on a tablet, blue light is emitted. This light messes with the body's production of melatonin, the hormone that regulates sleep. Melatonin tells our bodies it's time to wind down and rest. But blue light from screens disrupts this natural cycle, making it harder for kids to feel sleepy when they should.

Think about a child who's been playing a video game for hours before bed. They've likely experienced a surge of excitement or frustration, which already heightens their alertness. On top of that, the blue light exposure keeps them from feeling tired, further extending the time it takes to fall asleep. The result? Kids may struggle with poor sleep quality, longer time to fall asleep, and feeling groggy or irritable the next day. And when sleep patterns are consistently disrupted, it can lead to a cascade of other issues, including difficulty focusing in school, mood swings, and even problems with emotional regulation.

## The Brain's Developmental Window

It's important to note that children's brains are still developing, and their responses to screen time are different from those of adults. The prefrontal cortex, the part of the brain responsible for decision-making, impulse control, and understanding consequences, doesn't fully mature until the mid-20s. This means kids are more vulnerable to the effects of overstimulation, as they don't have the cognitive maturity to regulate their responses as well as adults do.

For example, a 6-year-old may become deeply immersed in a game and find it difficult to stop, even when it's time for bed or dinner. Their brain hasn't developed the capacity to shift attention or manage impulses in the way an adult's might. This is why younger children, especially, are more prone to overstimulation and a loss of control when it comes to screen use.

As they grow, children become better at managing their impulses, but the impact of early screen use can still linger. Studies have shown that excessive screen time during critical developmental windows can affect language acquisition, emotional regulation, and even social skills. For instance, a child who spends too much time on a device may miss out on important face-to-face interactions, which are essential for learning empathy and developing social awareness.

## Cognitive Effects: Focus, Attention, and Memory

While screen time can offer educational benefits, it also has its downsides in terms of cognitive development. The fast-paced nature of many digital activities, like video games or social media scrolling, can lead to difficulties with focus and attention. Research has suggested that children who spend more time on screens often exhibit shorter attention spans and more difficulty staying on task.

Take the example of a child who watches a fast-paced TV show with frequent scene changes. Their brain is being conditioned to expect constant novelty and stimulation. However, when they move away from screens-say, when they're asked to focus on homework-they may struggle to maintain that same level of engagement. The constant digital stimulation can make it harder for kids to concentrate on less stimulating, slower-paced tasks.

In addition, screen time can impact memory retention. The more time kids spend in front of screens, the less time they might spend engaging in activities that help build long-term memory, like reading, drawing, or interacting with peers. When kids do use screens for educational purposes, it's crucial that parents monitor the content to ensure it's enriching their cognitive abilities, rather than just offering passive entertainment.

**Physical Health and Posture**

Aside from the brain, screen time can also have physical consequences for children's bodies. Sitting for long periods in front of a screen can lead to poor posture, which, over time, can cause neck and back pain. With the rise of tablets and smartphones, children are often hunched over their devices, straining their muscles and eyes. The term "tech neck" has even been coined to describe the discomfort that comes from prolonged screen use.

Moreover, too much screen time can contribute to a sedentary lifestyle. Kids who spend hours in front of screens may not engage in enough physical activity, which can lead to weight gain, poor cardiovascular health, and a lack of muscle development. Parents often find themselves in a constant battle to encourage physical activity, and the allure of digital entertainment can make this even more difficult.

**A Case Study: The Thompson Family**

Let's consider a real-life example. The Thompson family has two kids, Emma and Jack, aged 10 and 13. From an early age, they limited screen time in the household, adhering strictly to the "no screens during meals or after 7 pm" rule. Over the years, Emma has developed a love for outdoor sports, and Jack spends his free time reading and drawing. However, there's an interesting twist: Despite the

Thompson's well-intentioned rules, Emma sometimes experiences "screen withdrawal" during weekends when they visit friends who have fewer restrictions on screen time. On those days, Emma finds it challenging to engage in other activities because she's so used to the instant gratification of screens.

This is a perfect example of how screen time affects children differently based on their exposure. While some kids, like Emma, thrive with limited screen time, others may become overly reliant on it for entertainment, making it harder to transition to other activities. It's not just about the time spent on screens, but the "quality" and "type" of content being consumed.

**What Parents Can Do ?**

Understanding these scientific underpinnings of screen time is just the first step. As a parent, it's essential to be proactive and mindful about how much screen time your child is exposed to. Balancing digital activities with offline experiences, ensuring they get adequate sleep, and encouraging physical activity are all important strategies to maintain healthy screen time habits.

Parents should also strive to model positive screen use behaviors. The more we lead by example, whether it's limiting our own screen time during family time or prioritizing outdoor activities, the better children will understand how to integrate digital tools into their lives responsibly.

## 1.2: Active vs. Passive Screen Use

In today's digital world, screen time is not just about how much time a child spends in front of a screen, but *how* they engage with it. Not all screen time is created equal. Some activities promote learning and creativity, while others lead to mindless scrolling and passive consumption. As a parent or caregiver, distinguishing between the two types of screen use is critical for fostering a healthy digital environment for children. In this subchapter, we'll explore the difference between active and passive screen use, shedding light on which types can be beneficial for children's development and which ones may be harmful in the long run.

**Active Screen Use: Engaging with Purpose**

Active screen use is where engagement happens on a deeper level. It's when a child interacts with the content in a way that requires them to think, create, or solve problems. These activities are typically more immersive and tend to stimulate the brain in ways that enhance learning, creativity, and critical thinking. Active screen time includes things like coding games, educational apps, interactive learning platforms, and even creative activities like digital drawing or video editing.

Take, for example, a game like **LightBot**, a programming game for kids. While it may look like just a fun puzzle, it teaches kids the basics of coding. The game requires children to use logic and problem-solving skills to guide a robot through a series of challenges. Instead of mindlessly tapping or watching, kids are actively engaged, learning to code concepts as they play. This is a great example of how screen time can be used to nurture essential skills like logical thinking, sequencing, and spatial awareness. It's engaging, purposeful, and, best of all, educational.

In a similar vein, apps like **Khan Academy Kids** are designed to turn learning into an interactive, fun experience. The app covers a range of subjects, math, reading, and even social-emotional learning, through engaging activities that prompt children to interact, solve problems, and think critically. This type of content is tailored to children's developmental stages, ensuring that their learning progresses as they explore the material. Here, the child isn't just absorbing information passively; they are actively participating in their educational journey.

**Case Study: The Garcia Family**

Let's take a closer look at the Garcia family, whose children have been introduced to both types of screen time. Maria, the youngest at 7, enjoys playing the game "**Osmo Coding Jam**" on an iPad. This app, designed to teach kids the fundamentals of coding through music, requires her to arrange blocks to create melodies. At first, it was a challenge, but Maria soon began to understand how the blocks worked together to form a harmonious tune, enhancing her cognitive skills and creativity. She not only learned to problem-solve, but also developed her interest in technology. Meanwhile, her brother, Daniel, spends a significant amount of time watching video clips on YouTube without much engagement. He goes from one video to the next, passively watching without much thought. Though both kids are using screens, the quality of their engagement couldn't be more different.

**Passive Screen Use: The Danger of Endless Scrolling**

On the flip side, passive screen use involves little to no interaction. Instead of thinking critically or engaging with the content, the user is simply consuming it. This is the type of screen use often associated with mindlessly scrolling through social media, watching endless episodes of TV shows, or binge-watching YouTube videos. There is little room for creativity or thought, and in many cases, the content doesn't require the child to do much of anything.

Endless scrolling, for instance, is a hallmark of many social media platforms. Instagram, TikTok, and even Facebook encourages this kind of passive consumption. The algorithms behind these platforms are designed to show users content they'll most likely click on, keeping them scrolling for longer periods. While there's nothing inherently wrong with watching a short video or two, spending hours on these platforms can lead to a lack of real-world engagement, social isolation, and, in some cases, a distorted sense of reality. Children, whose brains are still developing, may struggle to distinguish between what's real and what's simply entertainment.

The problem with passive screen use is that it offers no intellectual stimulation or emotional growth. It's easy to get sucked into watching videos that don't teach anything or improve cognitive skills. In fact, research has shown that excessive passive screen time can lead to a decrease in attention span, decreased social skills, and, over time, mental health issues like anxiety or depression. The more passive the content, the less likely children are to develop the critical thinking and problem-solving abilities they need in life.

**The Impact of Social Media on Children's Social Skills**

The rise of social media platforms like TikTok and Instagram has only amplified the effects of passive screen use. These platforms encourage passive consumption with short, often addictive content. Kids are exposed to a constant stream of images, videos, and ideas, which may seem harmless at first, but when combined with a lack of meaningful engagement, can start to take a toll.

For instance, a 13-year-old may spend hours scrolling through TikTok, watching dance challenges and comedic skits. While these videos may be entertaining, they don't contribute to emotional or cognitive development. The child isn't learning new skills, and the content frequently doesn't encourage much self-reflection. The longer they stay in this passive mode, the harder it becomes to shift gears and engage in more active, meaningful activities.

This type of content consumption can also impact social skills. Kids may spend more time online than in face-to-face interactions, which limits their ability to engage in real-world conversations or develop important social skills, like empathy, active listening, and conflict resolution. When a child spends too much time in front of a screen without meaningful engagement, they miss out on the critical, in-person experiences that help them navigate relationships in the real world.

**Striking a Balance: How to Foster Healthy Screen Habits**

While it's clear that some types of screen use are more beneficial than others, the key is balance. Just like with any other aspect of life, moderation is essential. Active screen time can be an excellent tool for learning, creativity, and skill-building, but it needs to be balanced with offline activities that encourage physical activity, social interaction, and emotional growth. Passive screen time, on the other hand, can be relaxing and enjoyable in small doses, but it should never dominate a child's day.

To foster healthy screen habits, parents should encourage kids to use screens for activities that require active engagement, like coding games, educational apps, or creative platforms, while setting firm boundaries around passive use. One strategy is the "**screen time contract**," where children agree to limit passive screen time in exchange for more active, meaningful engagement. For example, a child could be allowed 30 minutes of passive screen time after spending an hour working on a puzzle, drawing, or coding.

Parents should also model healthy screen habits themselves. If kids see their parents balancing screen time with other activities, they're more likely to follow suit. Taking time for outdoor play, family dinners without phones, or participating in creative projects together can set the tone for healthy screen time use in the home.

**Case Study: The Brooks Family's Balanced Approach**

Let's look at the Brooks family for another perspective. Sarah, 9, loves to create digital art on her tablet using a drawing app. She spends a portion of her screen time learning new techniques, experimenting with colors, and improving her skills. However, her parents make sure she gets enough offline time as well. After an hour of digital drawing, they encourage her to step outside and play soccer with her brother. They also set limits on TV time, making sure Sarah watches shows that are educational rather than just entertainment. This balance allows Sarah to enjoy the benefits of screen time, creativity, learning, and fun, while ensuring she's not missing out on essential offline activities.

To conclude, the line between active and passive screen use is crucial to understand when considering a child's digital habits. By promoting active engagement through educational games, creative activities, and learning apps, and limiting passive consumption, parents can ensure their children are making the most out of their screen time. By striking the right balance, children can harness the power of technology to enhance their learning and creativity without falling prey to the negative effects of passive screen use.

## 1.3: Developmental Stages and Guidelines

Understanding the impact of screen time on a child's brain and development is more complex than simply counting hours spent in front of a device. The age of a child plays a significant role in how they interact with and are affected by screens. The developing brain is uniquely vulnerable during certain stages, and screen exposure during these periods can either enhance or hinder growth, depending on how it’s used. Whether it's a baby's first interactions with a screen, a toddler's love for interactive games, a school-age child's immersion in educational apps, or a teenager's online social life, the effects are profound. Let’s break down the key developmental stages, providing age-specific guidelines for healthy screen exposure.

**Infants: The First 18 Months**

The earliest stage of life, infancy, is when the foundation for brain development is laid. In these first months and years, babies’ brains grow at an astounding rate, making it an essential period for sensory and motor skill development. During this time, the brain is most receptive to learning from physical interaction with the environment, including talking, touching, and exploring. The American Academy of Pediatrics (AAP) strongly recommends that children under 18 months avoid screen time altogether, except for video chatting with family or close friends. The key reason behind this recommendation is that infants learn best from real-life experiences and human interaction, not from passively viewing images or videos on a screen.

For example, when an infant is held in a caregiver's arms and shown different objects, they begin to understand the world through direct sensory experiences. Their brain forms connections as they touch, smell, and hear things. Exposing an infant to screens too early can disrupt this process, potentially delaying their language development and cognitive abilities. Babies who spend a lot of time looking at a screen miss out on crucial face-to-face interactions and physical exploration, both of which are vital for their early development.

Case in point: the O'Connor family made a decision early on to keep their baby, Ella, screen-free until she reached her first birthday. Instead of watching videos or using apps, they engaged her with books, interactive toys, and, most importantly, meaningful one-on-one conversations. As a result, Ella reached her early milestones, like saying her first words, on schedule, and she exhibited a strong ability to connect with people through eye contact and laughter.

**Toddlers: 18 Months to 3 Years**

As toddlers approach the 18-month mark, they start to explore more complex interactions. Their growing curiosity about the world leads them to seek new information, often through play and experimentation. It's also around this time that parents may begin to introduce limited screen time. The AAP recommends no more than one hour per day of high-quality, interactive content for children aged 18 months to 3 years. The key word here is "interactive." Content that requires toddlers to participate, think, and move, such as educational apps or games, can be beneficial when used in moderation.

For instance, **PBS Kids** has developed a variety of apps and shows that promote learning in areas like math, reading, and social-emotional development. These programs frequently involve characters who guide children through simple activities, like counting or identifying colors, which can be a valuable tool for enhancing early learning. However, passive screen activities, such as watching a TV show without any interaction, don't offer the same benefits.

The danger with excessive screen time during the toddler years lies in the potential for social and emotional development delays. If a toddler spends too much time looking at a screen and not enough time interacting with people, they may miss critical developmental cues, like learning to read facial expressions, understand tone, or develop empathy.

For example, 2-year-old Lucas became obsessed with watching cartoons on his tablet. His parents soon noticed that he became less interested in interacting with family members and had trouble expressing his emotions. Once they reduced his screen time and encouraged more face-to-face play, Lucas regained interest in social interactions and his language skills improved dramatically.

**School-Age Children: 6 to 12 Years**

As children enter school age, the role of screen time evolves. By this stage, they are not only using screens for entertainment but also for learning. Educational games, videos, and apps can supplement their academic development, fostering skills in subjects like mathematics, science, and language arts. However, the AAP suggests that for children aged 6 to 12 years, parents should place consistent limits on screen time to ensure a healthy balance between virtual and real-world activities. The recommendation is no more than two hours per day of recreational screen use.

While it might sound restrictive, the two-hour guideline isn't meant to be punitive, it's designed to encourage children to explore hobbies and interests outside of screens. Kids who spend too much time with digital devices may be more prone to sedentary behaviors, like sitting for hours at a time. It's important to integrate physical activity, creativity, and social interaction into their routines, even if it means stepping away from a game or show for a while.

An excellent example of how school-age children can benefit from screen time is through the use of educational apps like "**Duolingo**" or "**Scratch**". Duolingo allows kids to learn a new language at their own pace, while Scratch teaches basic coding by allowing kids to create their own interactive stories and games.

These types of apps offer opportunities for active engagement and skill-building, rather than just passive consumption.

Let's look at the Johnson family: their daughter, Sophie, is 8 years old and loves both science and video games. Her parents found an app called "**Mystery Science**", which provides interactive lessons on various scientific topics in a fun and engaging way. Instead of just watching videos, Sophie could explore, experiment, and answer questions, making her learning experience both immersive and educational. At the same time, Sophie also plays soccer twice a week, helping her stay active and engaged with her peers. By maintaining this balance, Sophie benefits from both her screen time and the offline activities that enrich her development.

**Teenagers: 13 to 18 Years**

Teenagers are at a critical stage in their development. They are refining their cognitive abilities, forming their identities, and navigating increasingly complex social landscapes. Screen time, particularly social media, plays a significant role in how teenagers interact with the world. However, excessive use can interfere with their emotional well-being, sleep patterns, and face-to-face social skills. The AAP advises that parents continue to set consistent limits on screen time for teenagers and encourage healthy sleep habits. Teens should be especially mindful of how screens, especially blue light from phones, tablets, and computers, can interfere with sleep cycles.

The challenge with screen time for teenagers is its social component. Social media apps like "**Instagram**", "**Snapchat**", and "**TikTok**" can be a source of connection, but they can also create pressure to conform to unrealistic standards of beauty, success, and popularity. This pressure can lead to mental health issues like anxiety, depression, and body dysmorphia. To mitigate these risks, parents, and teens should have open conversations about healthy screen use and set boundaries around online activities. Teens benefit from having structured time away from screens, whether that's during family dinners, study sessions, or at least one tech-free hour before bed to improve sleep quality.

Take 15-year-old Mia, for example. She's an avid social media user and spends a significant amount of time scrolling through Instagram and TikTok. However, her parents noticed that her mood was often down after long hours of online interaction, and she was struggling with sleep. After a family discussion, they agreed to set some boundaries. Mia now has an hour of screen time before dinner and is allowed to check social media only after completing her homework. The new routine helped Mia improve her sleep habits and reduce anxiety, while still allowing her to stay connected with friends.

**A Holistic Approach to Screen Time**

Each developmental stage requires different considerations when it comes to screen exposure. From infancy through the teenage years, the impact of screen time varies, and so should the guidelines for use. By following age-specific recommendations and being mindful of developmental windows, parents can ensure that screen time enhances their child's growth rather than hindering it. The goal isn't to eliminate screens, but to integrate them in a way that promotes learning, creativity, and healthy development.

By making informed decisions, setting boundaries, and fostering a balance between screen time and real-world experiences, parents can help their children navigate the digital age with confidence, awareness, and healthy habits.

## 1.4: Screen-Time Myths Debunked

In today's digital age, screen time often gets a bad rap. The words "screen time" are frequently associated with negative consequences, from harming kids' health to impeding their social skills. However, not all screen time is created equal. The truth lies somewhere in between the extremes of total avoidance and reckless indulgence. Let's take a closer look at some of the most common myths about screen time and set the record straight.

**Myth 1: All Screen Time Is Bad for Kids**

One of the most pervasive myths is that any screen exposure is harmful to children. While it's true that excessive screen time can lead to negative outcomes-such as poor sleep, physical inactivity, and social isolation-it's not all bad. In fact, there are plenty of instances where screen time can be educational, enriching, and beneficial to kids' development.

Take "**educational apps**" like "**Khan Academy Kids**", which offers interactive learning experiences for young children. These apps can stimulate cognitive development, teach problem-solving, and introduce children to complex ideas in an engaging way. The same goes for video games that require strategy, teamwork, and critical thinking, which can enhance skills that are useful in both school and everyday life.

Let's talk about Emma, a 7-year-old who struggled with math. Her parents introduced her to a learning app that gamified addition and subtraction. Through the app, Emma not only improved her math skills but also developed a love for learning. The app allowed her to progress at her own pace, making screen time both beneficial and productive. If Emma had been limited to a blanket "no screen time" rule, she would have missed out on a valuable educational tool.

The key takeaway here is the importance of intentionality. Screen time becomes problematic when it's unstructured or when it's used as a mindless activity. If the content is purposeful and educational, it can contribute to a child's learning and growth. The problem isn't screens themselves, it's how they're used.

**Myth 2: Screen Time Causes Bad Behavior and Aggression**

Another myth that often circulates is the belief that screen time, especially violent video games or TV shows, leads to aggression and behavioral issues. While studies have shown a correlation between exposure to violent media and short-term increases in aggression, it's not as straightforward as some make it out to be. Not all screen content has the same impact, and the effects can vary widely depending on the individual child's temperament and the amount of time spent engaging with certain types of media.

For example, research on the effects of violent video games has shown that children who already have a tendency toward aggression may become more irritable when exposed to violent content. However, children with a more peaceful disposition may not exhibit the same behaviors after playing similar games. Additionally, factors like parental involvement, supervision, and discussions about the content can significantly influence how a child responds.

Consider Liam, a 10-year-old who enjoys playing competitive online games. While some of the games he plays involve combat or strategy, his parents monitor his gaming time and encourage him to play with friends rather than alone. They also ensure he balances his time with outdoor activities, reading, and socializing with peers. As a result, Liam has learned how to manage his emotions, communicate effectively with others, and stay calm under pressure. The problem wouldn't lie in the screen time itself, but rather in the absence of guidance and moderation.

To combat the myth that all screen time leads to negative behavior, it's crucial to recognize that the type of content, the child's age, and how parents manage and engage with screen use can all influence the outcome. Proactively setting limits, fostering open communication, and encouraging non-screen-based activities will ensure that screen time does not lead to problematic behavior.

## Myth 3: Too Much Screen Time Will Make Kids Lazy and Unhealthy

The myth that screen time leads directly to poor physical health or inactivity is rooted in the assumption that time spent in front of a screen automatically means no physical activity. This misconception fails to account for the growing trend of interactive fitness apps, "**active video games**", and educational platforms that encourage movement, like those that integrate "**augmented reality (AR)**".

Take "**Pokemon G**o", for example. This game encourages children and adults alike to get outside and walk in order to catch virtual creatures hidden in real-world locations. By using location-based AR technology, players have to physically move, increasing their steps and promoting exercise while having fun. In fact, many kids who play the game have reported walking more than they ever did before, contributing to their overall physical well-being.

In another example, "**Just Dance**", a dance game that uses motion sensors, requires players to mimic dance moves to stay in rhythm. It's not just fun; it's a form of exercise that can get kids up and moving, burning calories while they enjoy their favorite songs. This game combines the best of both worlds, engaging screen content and physical activity.

While sitting for long periods is undeniably unhealthy, it's crucial to recognize that "**not all screen time encourages a sedentary lifestyle**". It's the context and purpose behind the screen time that matters most. When combined with physical movement and active play, screens can be part of a balanced routine that supports both mental and physical health.

**Myth 4: Screen Time Ruins Social Skills**

Another common misconception is that screen time hinders a child's ability to develop strong social skills. People often worry that if kids are spending too much time on devices, they won't know how to interact with others in real life. However, this perspective ignores the fact that digital interactions can also facilitate meaningful social connections.

For instance, children who engage in "**online multiplayer games**" frequently form friendships with people from different backgrounds and regions. These interactions can help them develop "**teamwork, problem-solving, and communication skills**" that are essential in today's globalized world.

Take Ben, a 14-year-old who plays an online game with friends from various countries. While his parents were initially concerned about the amount of time Ben spent gaming, they later realized that he was practicing important communication skills, such as negotiating, collaborating, and resolving conflicts. Ben had built a network of friends who shared common interests, and he regularly communicated with them in a positive and supportive way. His ability to maintain online friendships enriched his social skills and his confidence in offline interactions.

Of course, face-to-face communication is still crucial, but digital interactions don't necessarily have to be detrimental. With proper guidance, children can learn how to balance online and offline relationships, developing a wide range of social skills in both settings.

### Myth 5: Young Children Don't Need Screens for Learning

Finally, some believe that young children are too young to benefit from screens and should focus entirely on physical, real-world interactions. While it's true that screen time should be limited for infants and toddlers, "**technology-based learning**" can be a valuable tool for children of all ages when used appropriately.

For example, the educational TV show "**Sesame Street**" has been shown to improve literacy and math skills in preschool-aged children. Its interactive and engaging format helps young viewers grasp basic concepts while keeping them entertained. Similarly, apps that teach coding, math, or languages can introduce young children to valuable skills that might otherwise be inaccessible.

However, the real key is "**balance**". It's essential to strike a healthy mix of screen time and real-world interaction, especially for younger children. Using screens for short, intentional periods of learning, while still ensuring ample time for physical activity, play, and socialization, can be a highly effective way to introduce children to new concepts and build their skills in a fun, engaging way.

### A Balanced Approach

The world of screens isn't black and white. Myths like "all screen time is bad" or "screen time causes aggression" may have some basis in truth, but they fail to account for the complexities of how screen time affects children. Whether it's enhancing learning, fostering social skills, or encouraging physical activity, screen time can be a useful tool when used mindfully and in moderation. As with many aspects of parenting, the key is finding a healthy balance that works for both the child and the family.

---

# Chapter 2: Building Healthy Tech Habits for Kids

We've all seen it, kids glued to screens, from tablets to smartphones, effortlessly navigating apps, games, and videos. While technology can be an incredible learning tool, it can also become a double-edged sword. Without the right guidance, excessive screen time can disrupt routines, alter sleep patterns, and affect mental and physical well-being. The question isn't whether to let kids use technology, it's about how to create a balanced, healthy relationship with it.

Building healthy tech habits for kids is not just about setting limits; it's about teaching them how to use screens purposefully and responsibly. It's about creating boundaries that foster creativity, learning, and social connection, while protecting them from the potential pitfalls of mindless consumption. By instilling a mindful approach to screen time, kids can learn to navigate the digital world with balance, turning tech from a distraction into a positive, productive force in their lives.

In this chapter, we'll explore how to introduce healthy screen time habits at every stage of your child's development. Whether it's establishing tech-free zones, encouraging educational apps, or setting screen time limits, we'll cover practical strategies to help kids build a healthy relationship with technology. The goal is simple: empower children to use screens in a way that enhances their growth and well-being, while ensuring tech doesn't take over.

Let's dive into how we can help kids develop strong, balanced habits with the tools and resources available to them today.

## 2.1: The Digital Diet

In the same way that a balanced diet nourishes the body, a balanced digital diet is essential for nurturing a child's mind. Just like we wouldn't expect a child to thrive on junk food alone, we can't expect them to flourish if their screen time is filled only with mindless scrolling or passive entertainment. What makes a balanced digital diet? It's all about quality, variety, and moderation, three principles that should guide how children interact with technology, much like the way we approach nutrition.

### Quality: What Are They Consuming?

Just as we think about the nutritional value of food, whether it's a fruit or a candy bar, we need to consider the value of digital content. Not all screen time is created equal. Imagine your child spending hours watching YouTube videos that don't engage their thinking or creativity. The digital equivalent of a candy bar, right? The content may be fun or even funny, but it lacks the cognitive stimulation required for growth. On the other hand, apps that teach coding, engage in creative problem-solving, or promote physical activity through virtual exercise can be compared to wholesome, nutrient-rich meals.

Let's look at an example. Fourteen-year-old Sam is a typical teen with a smartphone glued to his hand. Most of his screen time is spent scrolling through social media apps or binge-watching shows on streaming platforms. While some of this is okay, his screen time is often filled with low-quality content, posts that leave him feeling anxious, unproductive, or disconnected. Meanwhile, his friend, Maya, spends a similar amount of time on her tablet, but she also dedicates part of her day to learning to code through interactive games, creating short films, or practicing a new language using an educational app. Sam and Maya's experiences highlight the importance of quality in screen time. Even though they spend similar hours online, Maya's digital diet is far more enriching.

**Variety: Mixing It Up**

Just as a nutritious diet is made up of a variety of foods, fruits, vegetables, grains, proteins, a healthy digital diet includes a variety of screen activities. Too much of one thing, like hours spent watching TV or playing the same game over and over, can lead to a digital imbalance, leaving your child disengaged and stagnant. A varied digital diet exposes kids to different types of content that stimulate various aspects of their development.

For younger children, variety could mean a mix of educational apps, video calls with grandparents, storybooks, and age-appropriate games. A toddler might learn the alphabet through fun, interactive apps but also enjoy moments of screen-free playtime, helping them develop their motor skills and creativity. School-age children benefit from a variety of learning tools, like puzzle games, creative outlets (drawing apps, music composition), and even video content that educates them about science, history, or art. Teens, on the other hand, may need a balance between productivity and leisure: school assignments on digital platforms, creative hobbies (like digital art or music production), and socializing with friends online.

A great example of a balanced digital diet for a 6-year-old might look like this:

- 30 minutes of educational game time (math, reading, problem-solving)
- 20 minutes of digital storytelling (drawing or story-making apps)
- 15 minutes of video chatting with a friend or family member
- 30 minutes of screen-free creative play (building with blocks, drawing with markers)

In contrast, for a 13-year-old, the daily digital diet might look like this:

- 45 minutes of school-related screen time (research, assignments)
- 30 minutes of interactive learning (coding game or app)
- 30 minutes of social media or messaging with friends
- 1 hour of creative activity (video editing, music production, digital art)

By blending educational content, creative outlets, and social interaction, kids can enjoy the benefits of technology without overindulging in one specific area.

**Moderation: How Much is Too Much?**

Moderation is key in every aspect of life, and screen time is no exception. The American Academy of Pediatrics recommends limiting screen time for children aged 2 to 5 years to no more than one hour per day of high-quality content. For children aged 6 years and older, the focus should shift to ensuring that screen time doesn't interfere with other important activities, like sleep, physical activity, and face-to-face interactions. The goal is to find a balance where technology enhances, rather than takes over, a child's day-to-day life.

Let's put it into perspective. Nine-year-old Eli loves to play video games but finds himself often staying up late to finish "just one more level." The next morning, he struggles to wake up for school, his mood is low, and he has trouble focusing on class. The problem here isn't the games themselves, it's the lack of moderation. With some adjustments, like setting screen time limits or establishing tech-free zones like the dinner table or bedroom, Eli could learn how to manage his time better. Perhaps he could play games for 30 minutes after school, but switch to something more productive (like reading or doing homework) afterward.

A good rule of thumb is to allow screen time as a reward for completing other important activities. If Eli finishes his homework or reads for 30 minutes, he earns a set period of screen time. This teaches him the concept of moderation and self-regulation, helping him develop healthy tech habits that last a lifetime.

**Building a Digital Diet Template for Different Age Groups**

Now, let's break down what a "balanced digital diet" could look like across different age groups. It's essential to remember that these are flexible guidelines, not strict rules, and should be adapted based on the individual child's needs and interests.

- **Infants (0-2 years):** Screen time should be extremely limited at this stage. The focus should be on face-to-face interaction and sensory exploration. If screens are introduced, it should be for joint media engagement (i.e., watching something with a parent) and for short periods.
- **Toddlers (2-5 years)**: Screen time should still be limited to one hour or less per day, with content focused on learning and interaction. Apps or shows that teach numbers, letters, shapes, and simple concepts can be engaging. It's important that this time is interactive, watching a show together and discussing it, or playing an educational game that encourages participation.
- **School-Age Kids (6-12 years):** As children grow, their screen time needs to be balanced between educational activities and fun. The goal is to mix learning (interactive games, educational videos, online classes) with creative expression (drawing, music, writing). Limiting screen time in the evening can also help ensure children are getting the proper amount of sleep.
- **Teens (13-18 years):** Teens require a more nuanced approach. School assignments, socializing, and self-expression via digital platforms can take up a significant

portion of their day. However, moderation is key. Encouraging teens to balance their screen time with physical activities, hobbies, and in-person socialization is crucial for maintaining mental and physical health.

### Wrapping Up the Digital Diet Approach

A balanced digital diet doesn't just limit how much time a child spends on screens; it prioritizes the quality of that time and ensures a wide variety of activities. Quality, variety, and moderation aren't just buzzwords; they're the pillars that can help children develop a healthy relationship with technology. By creating an environment where screens are tools for growth, creativity, and connection, we can foster digital habits that enrich, rather than diminish, a child's life.

## 2.2: Choosing Age-Appropriate Content

Not all digital content is created equal. As parents and caregivers, selecting age-appropriate apps, games, and videos for kids can feel like navigating a cluttered store aisle without a clear map. That's where the idea of "Digital Nutrition Labels" comes in. Much like how food labels guide us in choosing healthy snacks over junk, digital nutrition helps evaluate content for its value, relevance, and potential impact on young minds. Knowing what to look for, and what to avoid, can make all the difference in fostering a positive digital experience.

### The Concept of Digital Nutrition Labels

Imagine if every app or game came with a clear label detailing its "ingredients", features, benefits, and potential drawbacks. While the industry hasn't standardized such a label yet, we can create our own framework for assessing digital content. Think of it like this: just as you might check a food label for sugar, fiber, or additives, you can evaluate digital content based on criteria like educational value, engagement level, and safety.

**Start by asking these questions**:

- **What's the purpose?** Does the app or game promote learning, creativity, or social interaction?
- **Is it age-appropriate?** Does the content match the developmental stage of the child?
- **Does it encourage active engagement?** Look for apps that require problem-solving, critical thinking, or interaction instead of passive consumption.
- **What are the privacy policies?** Ensure the app doesn't collect unnecessary data or expose children to advertising traps.

For example, take an app like "**Toca Life World**", which allows kids to explore, create, and role-play in a virtual world. It's a great example of positive digital nutrition, it fosters creativity, has no ads, and respects user privacy. Contrast this with some "**free**" apps that are riddled with pop-up ads, in-app purchases, and questionable content. The difference is like comparing a nutritious meal to a sugar-loaded snack.

**Red Flags to Watch Out For**

Not all flashy apps or popular games are as harmless as they seem. Some can undermine a child's emotional or cognitive well-being, so it's important to recognize the warning signs of harmful content. These red flags should prompt you to steer clear:

- **Aggressive or inappropriate themes:** Games with excessive violence, gambling, or overtly mature themes can desensitize children or expose them to concepts they're not ready to process.

- **Endless loops**: Apps designed to hook kids into repetitive cycles without a clear endpoint often lead to overuse.
- **Manipulative design**: Features like loot boxes, countdown timers, or endless notifications are designed to exploit human psychology for profit.
- **Lack of transparency**: Apps with vague descriptions or poor user reviews typically hide flaws, such as hidden charges or low-quality content.

Take the story of 10-year-old Ethan. His parents downloaded a seemingly harmless puzzle game for him. But as Ethan progressed, the game introduced costly "**power-ups**" required to complete levels, along with ads for other questionable apps. Frustrated and upset, Ethan's experience turned into a lesson for his parents, they realized the importance of vetting content beyond surface-level appeal.

**Tools for Assessing Quality**

Thankfully, there are reliable tools and strategies to help parents evaluate digital content effectively:

**1. Third-Party Review Platforms**

Websites like "**Common Sense Media**" or "**Family App Guide**" provide detailed reviews of apps, games, and videos. These platforms analyze content for age-appropriateness, educational value, and safety, offering peace of mind before you hit "**download**."

**2. Parental Control Apps**

Tools like "**Bark**" or "**Qustodio**" can monitor the content your child interacts with, providing insights into their digital habits and alerting you to inappropriate material.

**3. Trial Periods**

Whenever possible, try the app or game yourself before introducing it to your child. This firsthand experience can give you a sense of whether it aligns with your family's values.

**4. Content Ratings**

Pay attention to content ratings on app stores, but don't rely on them entirely. They're a good starting point, but deeper research often reveals nuances not captured by generic labels.

### Crafting a Digital Nutrition Checklist

To make the process even easier, here's a simple checklist you can use to evaluate content:

1. **Purpose**: Is it educational, creative, or recreational? Does it align with your child's interests?

2. **Safety**: Are there adequate parental controls? Does it respect user privacy?

3. **Engagement**: Does it encourage active participation, collaboration, or critical thinking?

4. **Monetization**: Are there hidden fees, ads, or in-app purchases?

5. **Age Suitability**: Is the tone, language, and imagery appropriate for your child's age group?

Consider the case of Sarah, a mom of two boys aged 6 and 10. When her kids asked to download a popular game, Sarah used this checklist. While the game was engaging, it included ads for violent content and had no clear educational value. Instead, she introduced her boys to a different app that encouraged teamwork and problem-solving, giving them a better overall experience.

## Creating Positive Habits Around Content Choices

While it's essential to select appropriate content, it's equally important to involve kids in the decision-making process. Teaching them how to evaluate digital content for themselves fosters independence and critical thinking.

For example, you might ask your child to explain why they want to download a particular app. Encourage them to research it and share their findings with you. This dialogue not only builds trust but also teaches them to think critically about their choices.

Another strategy is setting boundaries around content consumption. For instance, establish "tech-free zones" in your home, such as during meals or before bedtime. Creating these habits helps children understand that while technology is valuable, it's not the centerpiece of life.

## The Role of Educators and Developers

Content creators and educators also play a significant role in shaping the digital landscape for kids. Developers who prioritize meaningful, age-appropriate content contribute to healthier digital habits. Meanwhile, schools that incorporate media literacy into their curriculum empower students to navigate the online world confidently.

Take a moment to think about how these efforts come together. The collaboration between families, educators, and developers creates an ecosystem where kids can thrive digitally, equipping them with the tools they need to make informed decisions about the content they consume.

## Final Thoughts

Choosing age-appropriate content doesn't have to feel overwhelming. By thinking of digital content like food and applying the concept of "**Digital Nutrition Labels**," parents can confidently curate experiences that enrich rather than hinder a child's growth. With the right tools, awareness of red flags, and open communication, it's possible to build a digital environment that nurtures curiosity, creativity, and connection.

While selecting age-appropriate content is essential for fostering positive digital habits, parents also need to address the hidden risks children may encounter online. Beyond selecting the right apps and games, ensuring your child's safety from cyberbullying and harmful interactions is crucial in today's connected world.

### Cyberbullying and Online Safety: Protecting Kids in the Digital World

Let's face it, navigating the online world with kids feels like walking a tightrope. One wrong step, and you're deep into the murky waters of cyberbullying and online dangers. This issue isn't just a footnote; it's a headline, a non-negotiable focus for any parent raising a digital native.

So, what can you do? The key is to be proactive, intentional, and informed. Below, we'll dive into practical steps for identifying and managing cyberbullying, while also laying out habits that nurture safer online experiences.

### Spotting the Signs of Cyberbullying

Cyberbullying isn't always loud or obvious, it's often subtle and insidious. Here's how to stay ahead:

- **Changes in Behavior**: Is your child withdrawing, suddenly moody, or avoiding their devices? These might be red flags.
- **Unexplained Anxiety**: If they seem nervous after using their phone or computer, don't dismiss it as a bad day.
- **Social Isolation**: Are they pulling away from friends they were once close to? It could be the result of online harassment.

### Action Steps for Parents

Dealing with cyberbullying requires a mix of vigilance, communication, and action. Here's your blueprint:

1. **Open the Dialogue**: Create a space where your child feels safe sharing their experiences. Ask questions like:

    - "Have you seen or experienced anything online that upset you?"
    - "How are your friends treating you on social media?"

2. **Monitor Without Hovering**: Use parental controls to keep tabs on activity, but balance this with trust. The goal isn't to spy, it's to guide.

3. **Document Everything**: If bullying occurs, take screenshots and save messages. This documentation is crucial if you need to escalate the situation.

4. **Involve Schools and Platforms**: Most schools and social media platforms have anti-bullying policies. Report incidents immediately and follow up to ensure action is taken.

5. **Seek Professional Help**: If your child's mental health is affected, don't hesitate to involve a counselor or therapist.

### Building a Foundation for Online Safety

The best defense is a strong offense. Here are practical ways to help your kids develop habits that protect them online:

1. **Set Boundaries Early**: Teach kids to avoid sharing personal information, such as their full name, address, or school name, in any online space.

2. **Encourage Critical Thinking**: Role-play scenarios where they might encounter suspicious links or strangers online. Ask, "What would you do if…?"

**3. Create a "Pause Before You Post" Rule**: Teach kids to think twice before posting or responding to messages, especially when emotions are high.

**4. Stay Updated on Trends** : Be aware of new platforms and apps. The better you understand where your child spends time online, the more equipped you'll be to guide them.

**Real-World Example: Turning Challenges into Teachable Moments**

**Case Study**: When 12-year-old Emma started getting nasty messages on a group chat, she didn't know how to handle it. She told her mom, who calmly helped her document the messages and block the bullies. They also worked together to report the group to the platform. This moment turned into a powerful teaching opportunity about standing up for herself and leaning on trusted adults.

**Why This Matters**

The online world isn't going anywhere, but with the right tools, your child can navigate it safely and confidently. By addressing cyberbullying head-on and instilling strong digital habits, you're not just protecting your child, you're empowering them to thrive.

## 2.3: Role Modeling Healthy Tech Use

Children are like sponges, soaking up everything they see, hear, and experience. This includes how we interact with technology. Parents often focus on setting limits for their kids but overlook the fact that their own habits leave an indelible impression. Every notification you check during dinner, every scrolling session in the middle of family time, it all sends a silent but powerful message. Kids don't just listen to what we say; they mimic what we do.

If fostering balanced tech habits in your child is a goal, it starts with self-awareness and intentional behavior. Let's explore how parents can become role models of mindful tech use by setting limits for themselves, using technology with purpose, and demonstrating that screens are tools, not crutches.

### Monkey See, Monkey Do: How Children Mirror Tech Habits

When it comes to technology, your behavior creates the blueprint your child follows. Studies show that children who see their parents using phones excessively are more likely to develop similar habits. For example, a survey by "**Common Sense Media**" found that nearly half of parents acknowledge they spend too much time on their devices, and their kids notice.

Consider a typical evening scenario: you're on the couch, scrolling through emails or catching up on social media, while your child sits next to you. Even if you're not interacting, they're observing. When they grow up, they might associate downtime with screen time, simply because that's what they've always seen.

A powerful way to counter this pattern is to lead by example. Demonstrate balance by prioritizing face-to-face interactions, physical activity, or hobbies over screen time whenever possible. This not only reinforces healthy habits but also strengthens family bonds.

### Setting Personal Limits: The Ripple Effect

Before you can guide your child, it's important to examine your own relationship with technology. Are you guilty of checking your phone as soon as you wake up? Do you find yourself answering work emails during family dinner? Setting boundaries for your own tech use creates a foundation for your child to follow.

Take, for instance, Olivia, a working mom of two. She noticed her daughter imitating her habit of reaching for her phone first thing in the morning. Realizing this wasn't the behavior she wanted to pass on, Olivia started leaving her phone in another room at night.

Instead, she encouraged morning rituals like stretching or reading together. Over time, her daughter began mirroring these healthier habits.

### Intentional Tech Use: Quality Over Quantity

One of the most effective ways to role model healthy tech use is to show intentionality. This means using technology with a clear purpose, rather than as a reflex or distraction.

For example, instead of aimlessly scrolling through social media, use technology to connect with loved ones, learn something new, or plan family activities. Share your reasoning with your child: "*I'm using my phone to check the weather for our picnic tomorrow*" or "*I'm sending a message to Grandma to see how she's doing.*"

Intentionality also applies to entertainment. Watching a family movie together and discussing it afterward demonstrates how screens can be a shared, enriching experience rather than a solitary activity. By framing technology as a tool to enhance life-not replace it-you help your child see its value without becoming overly dependent on it.

### The Power of Tech-Free Zones

Creating tech-free spaces or times in your home sends a strong message about boundaries. These zones don't have to be drastic, simple rules like "*no phones at the dinner table*" or "*screens off an hour before bedtime*" can make a big difference.

Consider the story of Jason, a single dad juggling work and parenting. He found that both he and his son were spending too much time glued to screens after dinner. Jason implemented a rule: from 7 p.m. to bedtime, no devices allowed. Instead, they played board games, read books, or just talked about their day. This simple change transformed their evenings, fostering deeper connection and helping his son see that life outside of screens can be just as engaging.

### Acknowledging Slip-Ups: A Teachable Moment

No one is perfect, and there will be times when you slip up, maybe you catch yourself checking your phone during family time or zoning out in front of a screen. The key is to acknowledge these moments openly.

For example, if your child points out that you've been on your phone too much, use it as an opportunity for dialogue. You might say, "*You're right. I've been spending too much time on my phone today. Let's take a walk together*." This shows humility and accountability, teaching your child that it's okay to make mistakes as long as you're willing to correct them.

### Turning Mistakes Into Lessons

There's a memorable story about Sarah, a mother of three, who realized her kids were starting to resent her constant phone use during their weekend outings. When her youngest daughter said, "**Mom, you love your phone more than us**," it was a wake-up call. Instead of brushing it off, Sarah apologized and made a pact with her kids to leave her phone in the car during family outings. The change didn't just improve her relationship with her children; it also helped her appreciate the moments she might have otherwise missed.

### Encouraging Co-Use

Sometimes, the best way to teach balanced tech habits is to share in your child's digital experiences. Co-use involves engaging with your child in their tech-related activities, whether it's playing a video game together, exploring an educational app, or watching their favorite YouTube channel.

This approach has two benefits: it allows you to monitor the content they're consuming, and it creates opportunities for meaningful interaction. Plus, co-use helps children see that technology can be a shared experience rather than an isolating one.

For example, if your child enjoys a specific educational app like **Khan Academy Kids**, spend time exploring it with them. Ask questions, discuss what they're learning, and encourage them to teach you something new.

**Balancing Work and Family in a Digital World**

For parents who work from home or have demanding jobs, separating work tech from personal tech can be especially challenging. The key is to establish clear boundaries between work and family time.

One strategy is to create a designated workspace where all work-related tech use happens. When you step out of that space, leave your devices behind. This signals to your family, and to yourself, that you're fully present.

Another idea is to set specific "check-in" times for work emails or calls, ensuring the rest of your time is focused on your family. For instance, you might allocate 15 minutes after dinner to tie up loose ends, but after that, it's strictly family time.

**The Long-Term Payoff**

Modeling healthy tech habits isn't just about the present; it's an investment in your child's future. By demonstrating balance, intentionality, and boundaries, you're equipping them with the tools they'll need to navigate a tech-saturated world responsibly.

When children see their parents using technology as a tool rather than a crutch, they learn to approach it with the same mindset. Over time, these lessons will shape their habits, helping them maintain a healthy relationship with technology throughout their lives.

### A Final Thought

Every time you choose to prioritize connection, mindfulness, or creativity over mindless scrolling, you're teaching your child a valuable lesson about what really matters. Remember, it's not about being perfect; it's about being present and intentional.

## 2.4: Quick Wins for Parents: Daily Habits to Build Better Tech Use for the Whole Family

Balancing technology with family life can feel like a juggling act, especially when screens seem to dominate every corner of daily living. But creating healthier tech habits doesn't always require big overhauls or dramatic changes. Sometimes, the smallest tweaks to your routine can lead to big wins for everyone in the family. Let's dive into practical, bite-sized strategies that parents can implement right away to foster better technology use for themselves and their kids.

### Morning Rituals: Starting the Day on the Right Foot

The way your family starts the day sets the tone for everything that follows. Instead of reaching for phones or tablets first thing in the morning, establish tech-free morning routines. These could include simple activities like eating breakfast together, talking about plans for the day, or encouraging your kids to engage in creative play before school.

Take Sam and his eight-year-old son, Ben, for instance. Sam used to check emails while Ben played on his tablet every morning. After noticing how disconnected they were, Sam implemented a "no screens until after breakfast" rule. They began doing quick stretches and talking about their goals for the day. Not only did this strengthen their bond, but it also gave Ben a more focused start to his school day.

## Tech-Free Meals: Reclaiming Family Time

Meals are one of the few times during the day when everyone comes together, so why let screens interrupt these moments? Creating a "**no devices at the table**" rule is an easy way to encourage conversation and connection.

Case in point: Sarah, a mom of three, introduced a "**basket rule**." Every meal, family members dropped their phones into a basket on the kitchen counter. This small change led to more laughter and storytelling around the table. Plus, her kids started looking forward to these uninterrupted moments of connection.

To make it fun, you could even take turns sharing a highlight of the day or asking silly questions, like, "**If you could be any animal for a day, what would you be and why?**" These conversations are more memorable than anything happening on a screen.

## Family Screen Time Agreements

Instead of setting rigid rules that feel like punishments, involve your kids in creating a family screen time agreement. This could include deciding together on daily limits, choosing tech-free zones, and setting priorities for offline activities. When kids feel included in the decision-making, they're more likely to respect the boundaries.

For example, the Martinez family created a colorful poster listing their "**Tech Time Rules**." Everyone agreed to unplug during meals, limit recreational screen use to one hour on school nights, and spend at least 30 minutes outside every day. They hung the poster in the living room as a visible reminder, turning the guidelines into a shared family commitment.

## The Power of Daily Check-Ins

Technology often pulls us in different directions, making it easy to lose track of how much time we spend on screens. To combat this, set aside a few minutes each evening for a family tech check-in. Use this time to reflect on the day's screen use, discuss any challenges, and plan tech-free activities for the next day.

For instance, eight-year-old Lily told her parents during one such check-in that she felt left out when her friends talked about a game she wasn't allowed to play. Her parents used this moment to discuss why they set content restrictions and brainstorm alternative games that aligned with their values. This approach not only addressed Lily's feelings but also reinforced the importance of open communication.

**Encouraging Offline Hobbies**

Sometimes, screens become a default because other activities aren't readily available. By introducing and encouraging offline hobbies, you can create appealing alternatives to technology. Whether it's painting, baking, building with Legos, or gardening, finding something your child loves outside of screens can be a game-changer.

Consider Josh, a 10-year-old who spent hours glued to his tablet after school. His parents noticed his fascination with cars and encouraged him to start building model kits. Over time, Josh's tablet use decreased as he became more absorbed in his new hobby.

As a bonus, when parents join in on these activities, it creates additional opportunities for bonding. If your child enjoys drawing, sit down with them and sketch. If they're into sports, go outside and toss a ball around. These moments are as fulfilling as they are fun.

**Creating Wind-Down Routines**

Evenings can be a challenge when it comes to tech use, especially if your kids use screens to relax. However, too much screen time before bed can interfere with sleep quality. Establishing tech-free wind-down routines can help everyone in the family prepare for restful sleep.

For example, you could designate the hour before bedtime as a screen-free zone and fill it with calming activities like reading, journaling, or talking about the day. One family replaced their nightly TV time with a "gratitude circle," where each person shared something they were thankful for. This not only improved their sleep but also created a positive end to their day.

**Leaning on Tech for the Right Reasons**

Not all tech use is bad, some apps, and programs can actually help families connect or learn together. The key is to be intentional about how you use it. For example, schedule family movie nights or play cooperative video games that everyone enjoys. Use educational apps or tools to explore new topics as a family, like learning a language or trying science experiments.

The Brown family used a language-learning app to practice Spanish together. Each night, they competed to see who could earn the most points. This turned screen time into a shared, interactive experience instead of a solitary one.

**Leading by Example**

No list of quick wins would be complete without emphasizing the importance of parental behavior. Your kids watch everything you do, including how you interact with technology. If you're glued to your phone during family time, it's hard to convince them to put their devices down.

Start by setting limits for yourself, like putting your phone away during meals or turning off notifications in the evening. Share your goals with your kids, too. Saying, "**I'm trying to spend less time on my phone so I can be more present with you**," reinforces that everyone in the family is working toward better habits.

## Building Tech-Free Traditions

Creating family traditions that don't involve screens can be a great way to break the habit of turning to devices for entertainment. These traditions can be as simple as weekly game nights, nature walks, or Sunday morning pancake breakfasts.

The Johnsons started a "**Friday Fun Night**" where screens were swapped for board games and homemade pizza. Over time, this became a cherished family ritual, something their kids looked forward to every week.

## The Domino Effect of Small Changes

What makes these daily habits so effective is their cumulative impact. Each small step, whether it's a tech-free meal, a family walk, or a shared hobby, adds up over time, creating a more balanced relationship with technology.

By focusing on these quick wins, you're not just improving your family's tech habits; you're also fostering stronger connections, encouraging creativity, and prioritizing well-being. The results might not be immediate, but the long-term benefits are worth every effort.

---

# Chapter 3: Setting Boundaries and Limits

The digital world is vast and alluring, offering endless opportunities for connection, learning, and entertainment. But like any powerful tool, it requires guidance to prevent overuse or misuse. Setting boundaries and limits isn't about restriction; it's about creating a framework that helps your family use technology intentionally and with purpose.

Think of it like a well-designed playground. The fences don't hinder the fun, they keep everyone safe, ensuring that play remains enjoyable and balanced. Without boundaries, technology can easily overshadow other vital parts of life, like face-to-face conversations, outdoor adventures, or quiet moments of reflection.

But where do you draw the line? Every family is different, and setting the "right" boundaries requires understanding your unique needs and values. It's about more than just deciding how much screen time is acceptable. It's about determining when, where, and how technology serves your family's goals, not the other way around.

In this chapter, we'll explore practical strategies to establish boundaries that work. From identifying tech-free zones to developing time-management techniques, you'll discover tools that bring clarity and balance to your family's digital life. Each approach is designed to empower, not restrict, helping you build a healthier relationship with screens while nurturing the bonds that matter most.

By the time you finish this journey, you'll feel equipped to lead with confidence, creating a home where technology complements your values rather than competing with them. Let's redefine what it means to live alongside screens, on your terms.

## 3.1: Establishing Family Screen Rules

Creating family screen rules isn't just about setting limits, it's about fostering collaboration, trust, and mutual understanding. When kids feel involved in shaping the guidelines, they're more likely to respect them, seeing the rules as shared agreements rather than imposed restrictions. This approach turns boundaries into opportunities for growth and connection, helping your family develop a healthier relationship with technology.

### Why Family Screen Rules Matter?

Without clear rules, screen time can quickly spiral into chaos. Maybe it starts with a few extra minutes on a favorite game or a sneaky late-night scroll. Before you know it, screens dominate the household, leaving little room for meaningful conversations or quality time. Establishing thoughtful screen rules ensures technology enhances rather than disrupts family life.

Rules also teach kids essential life skills. By setting clear expectations, you're modeling the importance of balance, self-discipline, and prioritizing what matters most. These lessons extend far beyond screens, shaping their approach to school, relationships, and future challenges.

### Step-by-Step Guide to Crafting Screen-Time Agreements

#### 1. Start with a Family Meeting

Bring everyone together for an open discussion. Let each family member share their perspective on screen use, what they enjoy, what frustrates them, and where they think improvements could be made. This dialogue sets the stage for collaboration and ensures everyone feels heard.

**2. Identify Shared Goals**

Frame the conversation around your family's values. Maybe you want more face-to-face time, fewer arguments about devices, or better focus on homework. When kids understand the "**why**" behind the rules, they're more likely to embrace them.

**3. Define Specific Rules**

Keep your rules clear and actionable. Avoid vague guidelines like "**limit screen time**" and focus on specifics:

- No screens during meals.
- Devices must be put away 30 minutes before bedtime.
- Weekday gaming is limited to one hour.

Tailor the rules to suit your family's needs. Younger kids may require stricter time limits, while teens might benefit from agreements about appropriate content and online behavior.

**4. Write It Down**

Create a written agreement that everyone signs. This formalizes the rules and serves as a reference if conflicts arise. Display the agreement somewhere visible, like the fridge, to reinforce its importance.

**5. Build in Flexibility**

Life happens, and strict rules can sometimes feel stifling. Include room for exceptions, like extra screen time during vacations or for special projects. Flexibility shows kids that the rules are there to support, not control, their lives.

**6. Review and Adjust Regularly**

As kids grow and their needs change, so will your family's relationship with technology. Schedule periodic check-ins to evaluate what's working, what's not, and how the rules can evolve.

**Sample Family Tech Rules for Inspiration**

Here's an example of a simple, balanced screen-time agreement:

- **Morning Rule**: No screens before school or until chores are completed.
- **Homework First**: Screens are allowed after all schoolwork is done.
- **Dinner Rule**: All devices go into a basket during meals.
- **Bedtime Boundary**: Phones and tablets stay out of bedrooms overnight.
- **Shared Space Rule**: Online activities happen in common areas, not behind closed doors.

These rules are adaptable, feel free to tweak them to reflect your family's unique rhythm.

**Case Study: The Thompson Family's Digital Reset**

When Sarah and Mike Thompson noticed their two kids were spending hours glued to their devices, they knew it was time for a change. They held a family meeting to talk about their concerns and asked their children for input.

Their 10-year-old daughter suggested a rule for tech-free Sundays, where the whole family would spend the day hiking, cooking, or playing board games. Their 14-year-old son proposed a daily "**digital sunset**," where everyone, including the parents, powered down devices an hour before bed.

By involving their kids in the decision-making process, the Thompsons found the rules weren't met with resistance but enthusiasm. Over time, they noticed improved communication, more laughter around the dinner table, and better sleep for everyone.

### Navigating Pushback

It's natural for kids to test boundaries, especially when it comes to something as enticing as screens. The key is to stay consistent and compassionate. If a rule is broken, use it as an opportunity for conversation rather than punishment.

For example, if your child sneaks in extra gaming time, ask them why. Were they bored? Stressed? Understanding the "why" helps you address the root cause and refine the rules if necessary.

### Encouraging Accountability

Empower kids to take ownership of their tech use by involving them in tracking screen time or setting reminders for tech-free periods. There are plenty of apps that can help with this, turning rule-following into a fun, shared responsibility.

One family found success using a simple jar system. Every time someone followed a tech rule, they added a bead to a jar. Once the jar was full, the family celebrated with a special outing. This tangible reward system reinforced positive behavior and made the rules feel rewarding rather than restrictive.

### Building a Positive Tech Culture

Remember, the goal isn't to demonize screens, but to integrate them thoughtfully into your family's life. Celebrate the ways technology connects and inspires your family, like sharing funny videos, collaborating on a creative project, or exploring educational apps together.

By framing screen rules as a shared effort to enhance family life, you create a culture of respect, balance, and intentionality. This isn't about winning a battle over devices, it's about building a life where screens support, not overshadow, what matters most.

## 3.2: Creating Tech-Free Zones and Times

In a world where screens are everywhere, carving out spaces and moments free from technology can feel like reclaiming a bit of sanity. Tech-free zones and times aren't about rejecting technology, but about making room for deeper connections, uninterrupted rest, and meaningful activities that strengthen family bonds.

When implemented thoughtfully, these boundaries provide a healthy balance, showing kids that life offline is just as engaging, if not more so, than life on a screen. It's not about being rigid, but about creating intentional pauses in a fast-paced digital world.

### The Power of Tech-Free Meals

The dinner table is one of the simplest yet most powerful places to go tech-free. When phones and tablets are off the table, literally and figuratively, the focus shifts to conversation, laughter, and eye contact. This isn't just about eating together; it's about nourishing your relationships.

Research supports the idea that screen-free meals strengthen family bonds. Studies have shown that kids who regularly eat with their families tend to perform better academically, have better self-esteem, and are less likely to engage in risky behaviors.

**Example**: The Miller family found themselves struggling to connect amid their busy schedules. Their solution was simple: they declared the dining table a tech-free zone. At first, there was resistance, especially from their teenage son, who loved scrolling social media during dinner. But as the weeks went on, they noticed a shift. Mealtime became a space for storytelling, jokes, and even heated debates about whose turn it was to do the dishes.

To make tech-free meals a habit, consider these tips:

- Set clear expectations: Announce that mealtimes are for people, not devices.
- Create a phone basket: Have everyone place their phones in a basket before sitting down.
- Start small: If dinner every night feels overwhelming, begin with one or two meals a week.

**Declaring Bedrooms a Sanctuary**

Another transformative tech-free zone is the bedroom. Sleep is one of the first casualties of unrestricted screen use, especially for kids and teens. The blue light emitted by screens disrupts the body's natural sleep-wake cycle, making it harder to wind down and stay asleep.

By keeping screens out of bedrooms, you're promoting healthier sleep habits and creating a space for rest and relaxation. Encourage alternative bedtime routines, like reading a physical book, journaling, or simply chatting about the day.

**Case Study**: Eight-year-old Ellie was having trouble falling asleep and waking up grumpy. Her parents decided to ban devices from her bedroom, replacing her tablet time with a nightly ritual of reading a chapter from her favorite book together. Within weeks, Ellie was falling asleep faster, and her mornings were noticeably brighter.

To make this work, consistency is key. Lead by example by keeping your own devices out of your bedroom. Use a traditional alarm clock instead of relying on your phone, and create a charging station in a common area for everyone's devices.

### Carving Out Tech-Free Family Activities

Some of the best memories happen when everyone's fully present. Dedicating specific times for tech-free family activities helps foster stronger connections and creates opportunities for shared joy. Whether it's a weekly game night, a weekend hike, or a Sunday afternoon spent baking cookies, these moments remind everyone that life offline is rich and rewarding.

**Practical Suggestions:**

- **Game Night**: Dust off those board games or try out new ones that get everyone involved.
- **Outdoor Adventures**: Plan a family walk, picnic, or a trip to the local park.
- **Creative Projects**: Work on a puzzle, build something with LEGOs, or start a family art project.

**Anecdote**: The Johnsons made Saturday mornings their designated tech-free family time. At first, their kids were skeptical, grumbling about missing cartoons. But after a few weeks of pancake breakfasts, fort-building in the backyard, and impromptu dance parties, those mornings became the highlight of their week.

### Balancing Consistency and Flexibility

Setting tech-free zones and times works best when there's a balance between consistency and flexibility. Kids thrive on routines, but life isn't always predictable. There will be moments when a little extra screen time is necessary, like during a long road trip or while waiting at the doctor's office.

The key is to maintain the overall structure while allowing for occasional adjustments. This approach prevents the rules from feeling like a punishment and shows kids that boundaries are there to serve the family's well-being, not to stifle their freedom.

**Tip**: Use a family calendar to mark tech-free times, making them a visible and shared commitment.

### Common Challenges and How to Overcome Them

Implementing tech-free zones isn't always smooth sailing. Kids might resist, especially if they're used to constant access to screens. Here's how to navigate some common hurdles:

1. **Resistance**: Frame the rules as a family effort, not just something imposed on the kids. Emphasize the benefits for everyone.
2. **Forgotten Devices**: Create visual cues, like signs or baskets, to remind everyone of the tech-free zones.
3. **Exceptions**: Be clear about when and why exceptions are allowed, so they don't undermine the rules.

**Example**: The Park family faced pushback when they introduced tech-free evenings. Their solution was to tie the rule to a reward, anyone who stuck to the tech-free rule for a week got to choose the Friday night movie.

### Reaping the Benefits

Over time, tech-free zones and times create a ripple effect. Families report feeling more connected, kids show better focus and sleep patterns, and parents find themselves less stressed. These intentional breaks from technology bring clarity to what matters most: shared experiences, meaningful conversations, and the joy of simply being together.

As you experiment with these changes, remember that it's about progress, not perfection. Even small steps toward reducing screen time can lead to big changes in your family dynamic.

## 3.3: Conflict Resolution Strategies

It was a typical weekday evening at the Ramirez household. Dinner was over, the dishes were stacked in the sink, and 13-year-old Marcus was sprawled on the couch with his tablet. His mother, Carla, called out, "Time to log off, Marcus. Let's get your homework done."

"Just five more minutes!" Marcus groaned, not looking up from his game. Carla sighed. It was the third time she'd heard this plea that evening, and her patience was wearing thin. Yet, instead of snapping or grabbing the tablet, she paused, took a breath, and approached the situation differently.

This scenario is familiar to many parents, isn't it? Negotiating tech boundaries with kids and teens can feel like an uphill battle, but it doesn't have to be a source of constant tension. With the right strategies and tools, these moments can become opportunities to teach valuable lessons about respect, responsibility, and compromise.

### Understanding the Roots of Pushback

Before diving into strategies, it's essential to understand why kids and teens resist limits on their tech use. Screens are their social hubs, entertainment centers, and even their escape when life feels overwhelming. When you ask them to put devices away, it can feel like you're taking away more than just a gadget, it's their connection to the world.

Acknowledging this perspective doesn't mean caving to every request, but it sets the tone for a respectful conversation. It also helps to remember that conflict doesn't always mean defiance. Often, it's just their way of expressing frustration or testing boundaries, which is a normal part of growing up.

## Building a Foundation of Trust

To handle pushback effectively, you need a solid foundation of trust and mutual understanding. Kids are more likely to respect rules if they feel heard and valued. Start by involving them in the decision-making process around screen-time boundaries.

For example, sit down as a family and discuss why limits are necessary. Let your kids share their viewpoints too. A teenager might say, "I need my phone for group projects," or a younger child might mention their favorite show. Use this input to shape rules that feel fair while aligning with your family's values.

## Scripts for Common Scenarios

### Scenario 1: "Just 5 more minutes!"

**What to say**:

"I get it, you're really into what you're doing. Let's set a timer for five more minutes, but after that, the device needs to go away. If you turn it off without arguing, we'll have time for [insert a fun activity they enjoy]."

This approach acknowledges their feelings while offering a clear limit and a positive incentive. It also shifts the focus from what they're losing to what they'll gain by cooperating.

### Scenario 2: "But everyone else gets to!"

**What to say:**

"I know it seems like other kids don't have limits, but every family is different. In our family, we prioritize [insert a value like health, relationships, or education]. That's why we have these rules. Let's talk about how we can make them work better for you."

Here, you're reinforcing family values while inviting collaboration, which can reduce feelings of unfairness.

**Scenario 3: "Why do you get to use your phone all the time?"**

**What to say**:

"You're right, I use my phone a lot, and I can see how that feels unfair. Let's work on this together. Maybe we can have tech-free times where everyone, including me, puts devices away."

This script flips a potential argument into an opportunity to model the behavior you want to see, showing that rules apply to everyone.

**Tools for Managing Conflict**

When conflicts escalate, having the right tools can help diffuse tension.

1. **Timers and Alarms**: Set clear boundaries with timers. For instance, use a kitchen timer or app to signal the end of screen time, taking the pressure off you as the enforcer.

2. **Tech-Free Zones**: Establish areas like the dinner table or bedrooms where devices are off-limits, creating natural breaks from screens.

3. **Cooling-Off Periods**: If a disagreement spirals, give both yourself and your child time to cool down before revisiting the issue. This prevents arguments from becoming emotionally charged.

**Learning Through Real-Life Examples**

Take the Thompson family as another example. They struggled with their 10-year-old daughter, Lily, who often refused to log off her tablet. Instead of resorting to punishment, her parents implemented a family meeting. They explained why screen limits mattered, listened to Lily's feelings about her favorite apps, and then worked together to create a plan.

The result? A schedule where Lily got uninterrupted screen time during specific hours, followed by family activities like board games or walks. Because Lily helped design the plan, she was more willing to stick to it, and conflicts around screen time significantly decreased.

### The Importance of Consistency

Consistency is the backbone of effective conflict resolution. If rules change constantly or are only enforced sporadically, kids will naturally push boundaries to see what they can get away with.

That doesn't mean being rigid, though. Life happens, vacations, special events, or even a tough day at school might call for a bit more flexibility. The key is communicating these exceptions clearly, so your kids understand they're not permanent changes.

### Building Long-Term Skills

Conflict resolution around tech use isn't just about managing devices, it's about teaching lifelong skills. When you handle pushback with empathy and firmness, your kids learn how to express themselves respectfully, negotiate compromises, and accept limits.

One parent shared how their teenager, initially resistant to screen limits, began setting their own boundaries after seeing how it improved their mood and grades. By staying consistent and modeling positive behavior, the parent turned conflicts into teachable moments.

### Wrapping It Up

Navigating pushback from kids and teens is never easy, but it doesn't have to be a constant struggle. By understanding their perspective, involving them in rule-setting, and responding with empathy, you can create an environment where tech boundaries are respected rather than resented.

When these strategies are applied consistently, they not only reduce arguments but also strengthen family bonds. And as your kids grow, the lessons they learn from these interactions will stick with them, shaping how they approach challenges far beyond screen time.

---

# Chapter 4: Tools and Resources for Parents

Parenting in the digital age feels like navigating an uncharted maze. The tools our parents relied on are no longer enough to guide us through a world dominated by algorithms, notifications, and endless scrolling. It's as though the rules of engagement have been rewritten, and as parents, we're left searching for a reliable compass.

But here's the thing: the right tools and resources can turn this challenge into an opportunity. They're not just crutches to lean on but powerful allies that equip us to create healthier habits, foster meaningful connections, and model intentional tech use. Whether it's a well-designed app, an insightful book, or a practical strategy, these resources bridge the gap between intention and action, giving us the confidence to lead by example.

Transitioning from theory to practice requires more than just knowledge; it demands accessible, adaptable solutions. This section aims to arm you with practical tools and actionable ideas, each carefully curated to address common challenges while fitting seamlessly into the rhythm of daily life.

Let's explore the tools that can transform how we approach parenting in a connected world, one meaningful step at a time.

## 4.1: Parental Controls and Monitoring Tools

It was a typical Thursday evening when Lisa noticed her 10-year-old son, Jake, glued to his tablet at the dinner table, again. Despite the family rule about no screens during meals, Jake seemed oblivious, lost in the world of online gaming. Lisa sighed, feeling the familiar twinge of frustration. She didn't want to be the nagging parent, but something had to give. That night, after Jake went to bed, she decided to explore parental control tools that could help her manage screen time without constant arguments.

Lisa's story is far from unique. Parents everywhere grapple with the delicate balance between setting boundaries and fostering trust in a digital age. Technology can feel like both a blessing and a curse, but with the right tools, it doesn't have to be a battle. Let's dive into how parental control and monitoring tools can be used effectively, ensuring they empower families rather than create rifts.

**Popular Tools: What They Offer and How They Compare**

The marketplace is flooded with apps and software claiming to help parents manage their kids' tech use, but not all tools are created equal. Below is a review of two of the most popular options, along with a comparison chart to highlight their features:

**1. Google Family Link**

Google Family Link is a free app that lets parents set screen time limits, approve or block app downloads, and monitor activity on their child's device. It's intuitive and integrates seamlessly with Android devices, though it also offers limited compatibility with iOS.

- **Strengths**: Easy to use, robust activity reports, free.
- **Limitations**: Limited iOS functionality, no content filtering for web browsing.

**2. Qustodio**

Qustodio is a more comprehensive tool that provides content filtering, screen time controls, and even location tracking. It works across multiple platforms, including Windows, Mac, Android, and iOS, making it versatile for families with diverse tech ecosystems.

- **Strengths**: Advanced content filtering, multi-platform compatibility, location tracking.

- **Limitations**: Subscription-based, can be overwhelming for beginners.

**Comparison Chart: Key Features**

| Feature | Google Family Link | Qustodio |
|---|---|---|
| **Cost** | Free | Subscription-based |
| **Screen Time Limits** | Yes | Yes |
| **Content Filtering** | No | Yes |
| **Cross-Platform Support** | Limited | Extensive |
| **Ease of Use** | High | Moderate |
| **Activity Reports** | Basic | Detailed |

**Tips for Setting Up Controls Without Breaking Trust**

Setting up parental controls is more than just downloading an app or tweaking a setting. It's about creating a system that feels collaborative rather than authoritarian. Here are practical tips to ensure your approach fosters trust:

**1. Involve Your Kids in the Process**

Transparency goes a long way. Instead of sneaking in restrictions, have an open conversation with your child about why these tools are necessary. Frame the discussion around safety, balance, and responsibility rather than punishment.

- **Example**: *"We're going to try this tool to help us all stay more mindful about how we use our devices. What do you think about setting a two-hour daily limit for gaming?"*

**2. Customize Settings to Fit Individual Needs**

Not all kids use technology the same way. Tailor settings to suit your child's habits and maturity level. For instance, a teenager might need social media time limits, while a younger child might benefit from stricter content filtering.

**3. Use Controls as Guardrails, Not Walls**

Parental controls should guide behavior, not replace the need for conversation and education. Encourage self-regulation by discussing why certain boundaries exist and how they can make better choices.

- **Anecdote**: One family implemented time limits for YouTube but also taught their kids how to identify credible content versus clickbait. Over time, the kids started self-monitoring their viewing habits.

**Common Concerns: "*Won't This Damage Our Relationship*?"**

It's natural to worry about pushback from kids when implementing these tools. However, when done thoughtfully, parental controls can strengthen relationships by reducing power struggles.

**Case Study: The "5 More Minutes" Dilemma**

Every parent has heard it: "Just 5 more minutes!" Instead of engaging in a tug-of-war, one family used Google Family Link to set a firm limit on gaming. When the time was up, the app gently notified the child, ending the session without the parent needing to intervene.

By pairing this with an agreement that any unfinished games could resume the next day, they found their child became more accepting of the rules over time.

**The Balance Between Consistency and Flexibility**

While consistency is key to making these tools effective, rigidity can backfire. Kids are more likely to respect boundaries if they feel there's room for negotiation when appropriate.

**Practical Example: Movie Night Exception**

A family that uses Qustodio decided to loosen screen time limits on Friday nights for a weekly movie tradition. This flexibility reinforced the idea that boundaries are there to support, not stifle, family time.

**Encouraging Responsibility**

Flexibility can also be a teaching moment. Offer opportunities for kids to earn additional screen time through chores or positive behavior, showing them how responsibility leads to rewards.

**Looking Beyond Tools: The Bigger Picture**

No app or software can replace the importance of trust and communication. Parental controls are tools, not solutions. By pairing them with ongoing conversations and modeling healthy tech use yourself, you can create a family environment where technology supports growth and connection rather than causing conflict.

## 4.2: Teaching Online Safety and Privacy

It was just another Sunday afternoon when Sarah noticed her 13-year-old daughter, Mia, staring at her phone with a mix of curiosity and unease. "Mom," Mia began hesitantly, "a stranger messaged me on this app saying they're from school, but I don't know them. They're asking weird questions."

Sarah's heart skipped a beat. This wasn't the first time she'd warned Mia about online safety, but the conversation felt theoretical back then. Now, it was real. She sat beside Mia and calmly went through the messages. This moment became a turning point, not just for Mia, but for the family's approach to digital life.

Stories like Sarah's are increasingly common. As kids navigate an ever-connected world, parents face the daunting challenge of preparing them to handle online threats. Teaching online safety and privacy isn't just about rules; it's about empowering kids to think critically and make wise decisions.

## Understanding Online Threats

The internet is a powerful tool, but it comes with risks that kids and teens may not immediately recognize. Here's a breakdown of some common online threats and how to approach them.

### 1. Cyberbullying

Cyberbullying is when harassment or bullying occurs online through social media, gaming platforms, or messaging apps. Unlike traditional bullying, it can happen 24/7 and often feels inescapable.

- **Example**: A boy named Ethan became withdrawn after receiving mean comments on his gaming profile. His parents noticed the change and opened a dialogue, eventually helping him report the behavior to the platform and block the offenders.
- **How to Teach**: Encourage kids to speak up if they experience or witness cyberbullying. Teach them how to use blocking and reporting features on apps.

**2. Phishing and Scams**

Phishing scams trick users into sharing personal information like passwords or financial details by pretending to be legitimate organizations.

- **Example**: A 12-year-old received an email claiming she'd won a gift card and needed to click a link to claim it. Fortunately, her parents had explained phishing scams, so she deleted it without hesitation.
- **How to Teach**: Explain that legitimate companies won't ask for sensitive information via email or direct messages. Teach kids to double-check website URLs and avoid clicking on suspicious links.

**3. Oversharing**

Kids may not realize that sharing personal details like their school name or daily routines can expose them to risks.

- **Example**: A girl who frequently posted about her dance classes unintentionally revealed her location. After a stranger began commenting on her posts, her parents stepped in to adjust her privacy settings.
- **How to Teach**: Talk about what's safe to share online and what's not. Use simple analogies, like treating personal information the same way they'd treat their house keys, something not to give away easily.

## Tips for Starting the Online Safety Conversation

Many parents struggle with how to approach this topic without sounding like they're lecturing. Here are some practical steps:

**1. Use Real-Life Scenarios**

Bring up age-appropriate examples of online risks. For younger kids, frame it as a story about "what if someone tried to trick you."

With older kids, share news stories or personal anecdotes to make the conversation relatable.

**2. Make It a Dialogue, Not a Monologue**

Instead of listing rules, ask open-ended questions to gauge your child's understanding and opinions. For example, "What would you do if someone asked for your password?"

**3. Keep the Tone Positive**

Online safety isn't about scaring kids; it's about equipping them with tools to navigate the digital world confidently. Celebrate when they make good decisions, like reporting suspicious activity or recognizing a scam.

**Building Practical Skills**

Empowering kids requires more than just talking, it's about teaching actionable steps they can take in different situations.

**Checklist for Internet Safety Talks**

**Use this checklist to guide your conversations:**

1. **Passwords:**
    - Teach the importance of strong, unique passwords.
    - Introduce password managers if age-appropriate.
2. **Privacy Settings:**
    - Show them how to adjust privacy settings on apps and platforms.
    - Explain the difference between public and private accounts.
3. **Recognizing Red Flags:**
    - Discuss warning signs of scams or phishing attempts.

- Teach them to verify emails or links with a trusted adult.

4. **Social Media Etiquette:**
   - Highlight the importance of kindness and respect online.
   - Discuss the permanence of digital footprints.
5. **Reporting and Blocking:**
   - Walk them through how to block users or report inappropriate content.
   - Encourage them to share concerns with you or another trusted adult.
6. **Critical Thinking:**
   - Teach them to question the validity of what they see online.
   - Discuss fake news, edited photos, and other forms of misinformation.

### Case Study: Turning Lessons into Habits

One family implemented weekly "tech talks" during dinner. Each week, they tackled a different topic, like recognizing scams or setting strong passwords. The kids began looking forward to these discussions, even bringing their own questions and examples from school or social media. Over time, this routine not only improved their online habits but also strengthened family communication.

### Adapting to Different Ages and Stages

Online safety isn't one-size-fits-all. Here's how to tailor your approach:

- **For Young Kids**:
  Focus on simple concepts like "not talking to strangers" and "asking permission before clicking."
  - **Example**: A mom explained online privacy to her 7-year-old by comparing it to keeping their home address a secret from strangers.
- **For Preteens**:
  Dive deeper into topics like phishing, online etiquette, and the dangers of oversharing.
  - **Example**: A dad role-played phishing scenarios with his 11-year-old to help her recognize suspicious messages.
- **For Teens**:
  Encourage discussions about digital footprints, reputation, and cyberbullying. Give them more autonomy while being available for guidance.
  - **Example**: A teen learned to manage her social media privacy settings after her parents showed her examples of how oversharing affected others.

**Building a Safety-First Mindset**

Teaching online safety isn't a one-time event; it's an ongoing conversation. Kids need to see that the internet can be a positive space when used wisely. By staying engaged, modeling good behavior, and keeping lines of communication open, parents can help their kids navigate the digital world with confidence.

## 4.3: Understanding Emerging Technologies

It started innocently enough. Jenna's 10-year-old son, Caleb, came running into the kitchen, clutching the family's smart speaker. "Mom, look! Alexa helped me solve my math homework!" His excitement was contagious, but Jenna couldn't ignore the nagging question in the back of her mind: was Caleb learning or simply outsourcing his thinking to AI?

That moment sparked Jenna's deep dive into the emerging technologies shaping her son's world. Artificial intelligence, virtual reality, and smart devices weren't just buzzwords, they were becoming integral to daily life. For parents like Jenna, understanding these tools wasn't just optional; it was essential for guiding kids toward safe and balanced usage.

**AI and Children's Interactions: The Double-Edged Sword**

Artificial intelligence (AI) is rapidly transforming how children learn and interact. From virtual tutors to personalized educational apps, the benefits are undeniable. Yet, the risks are equally important to consider.

**The Benefits**

AI can enhance children's learning experiences in ways that were unimaginable a decade ago. Adaptive learning platforms like Dream Box and Duolingo adjust lessons to a child's pace, making learning feel intuitive and engaging. AI-driven storytelling apps can even help kids develop creativity by co-authoring stories.

- **Example**: Take Ethan, a 9-year-old struggling with reading. His parents introduced him to an AI-powered app that used games and interactive lessons to improve his skills. Within months, Ethan's confidence soared, and his grades followed suit.

AI also makes life easier for parents. Tools like Google Assistant can set reminders for chores or read bedtime stories when schedules get tight.

### The Risks

However, relying too much on AI can stifle critical thinking and problem-solving. Caleb's excitement about Alexa solving his homework highlights this pitfall. Children might grow dependent on instant answers instead of developing the skills to tackle challenges independently.

Privacy is another major concern. Many AI tools collect data to improve performance, but how this data is stored and used can raise red flags. Parents should vet apps and devices carefully, ensuring they comply with strict privacy standards.

### Tips for Parents

1. **Balance is Key**: Use AI as a supplement, not a replacement, for traditional learning methods.

2. **Monitor Usage**: Regularly review how your child interacts with AI tools.

3. **Teach Awareness**: Explain to kids that AI isn't infallible, and encourage them to verify information from reliable sources.

## Virtual and Augmented Reality: Immersive Worlds with Real Impacts

Virtual reality (VR) and augmented reality (AR) are no longer confined to gaming. These technologies are being used in education, therapy, and even social interactions. But knowing when and how to introduce them to children is crucial.

### The Promise of VR and AR

VR and AR can make learning come alive. Imagine exploring ancient civilizations through a VR headset or using AR to dissect a virtual frog in biology class. These immersive experiences can spark curiosity and deepen understanding.

- **Example**: Sophia, a middle schooler fascinated by space, used a VR app to "visit" the International Space Station. The experience solidified her interest in science and motivated her to join her school's robotics team.

AR, in particular, blends the digital and physical worlds seamlessly. Apps like Google Lens allow kids to identify plants and animals on nature walks, making learning interactive and fun.

### The Challenges

Despite their benefits, VR and AR come with risks. Excessive use can lead to physical issues like eye strain or motion sickness. More concerningly, these technologies can blur the line between reality and fantasy, especially for younger kids.

Another concern is the content itself. VR and AR apps vary widely in quality and appropriateness. Parents need to ensure that the experiences are age-appropriate and align with their family's values.

### Introducing VR and AR Responsibly

1. **Start Small**: Begin with short, age-appropriate sessions to gauge your child's reaction.

2. **Set Boundaries**: Establish clear time limits and breaks to avoid overuse.

3. **Curate Content**: Research apps and experiences before introducing them to your child.

## Smart Devices and IoT: Managing Digital Ecosystems at Home

The Internet of Things (IoT) has revolutionized homes, turning ordinary devices into smart companions. From voice-controlled thermostats to connected doorbells, these tools add convenience, but they also raise unique challenges for families.

### Creating a Connected, Safe Home

Smart devices like Amazon Echo and Google Nest have become staples in many households. They can play music, set reminders, and even help with school projects. But managing these devices effectively requires foresight.

- **Case Study**: The Rivera family used smart plugs to manage screen time. When their kids reached their daily limit, the plugs automatically shut off power to gaming consoles and TVs. This approach encouraged healthier habits without arguments.

### The Risks of Over-Connectivity

While smart devices simplify tasks, they also increase the number of entry points for potential cyberattacks. Hackers can exploit poorly secured IoT devices to access personal information or even control home systems.

Another issue is data collection. Many devices record interactions to improve functionality, raising concerns about privacy.

### Building a Safe IoT Environment

1. **Secure Your Network**: Use strong, unique passwords for your Wi-Fi and IoT devices.

2. **Update Regularly**: Keep firmware up-to-date to protect against vulnerabilities.

3. **Educate the Family**: Teach everyone in the household how to use devices responsibly and recognize potential risks.

### Bringing It All Together

Emerging technologies are here to stay, and they're evolving faster than ever. For parents, the key is striking a balance between embracing innovation and protecting kids from its downsides. Whether it's guiding interactions with AI, introducing VR and AR thoughtfully, or managing a smart home ecosystem, staying informed is half the battle.

These tools can enhance your child's world, opening doors to creativity and learning. But they also demand careful navigation. With the right approach, you can help your family thrive in this tech-driven age while safeguarding what matters most.

## 4.4: Practical Tools and Templates: Turning Advice into Action

Managing screen time isn't just about knowing what to do, it's about having the right tools at your fingertips. Parents today need more than theory, they need ready-to-use templates, guides, and resources that fit into their busy lives.

This section bridges the gap between good intentions and lasting results by providing actionable tools that empower parents to create a healthy digital environment at home.

### Why Tools Matter ?

Advice inspires change, but tools drive action. A well-crafted screen time contract, a simple tech log, or a curated list of educational apps can turn everyday tech struggles into manageable routines. Templates set clear expectations, build consistency, and involve children in creating a sustainable digital balance. It's not about perfection, it's about creating a system that works.

## Actionable Tools for Every Family

### 1. Family Screen Time Contract

**Why It Works:**
Setting clear expectations together creates accountability, reduces arguments, and promotes cooperation.

**How to Use It:**
Gather as a family and create a personalized contract that outlines tech rules in a positive, collaborative way. This agreement makes everyone feel invested and heard.

**Family Screen Time Contract Template**

**Purpose:** This contract sets clear guidelines for technology use in our home, ensuring balance, respect, and healthy digital habits for every family member.

**What to Include:**

**1. Daily Screen Time Limits:**

- Weekdays: ________________ (e.g., 1 hour of leisure screen time after homework)
- Weekends: ________________ (e.g., 2 hours of leisure screen time)

**2. Tech-Free Zones:**

- 🏠 Bedrooms: **Yes / No**
- 🍽 Dinner Table: **Yes / No**
- 🚗 Car Rides: **Yes / No**
- 🌳 Outdoor Play Areas: **Yes / No**

**3. Approved Apps & Content:**

- Educational Apps: ________________________________
- Approved Games: ________________________________
- Streaming Services: ________________________________

**4. Online Safety Rules:**

- Never share personal information (address, school, phone number).
- Use respectful language online.
- Only connect with people we know in real life.
- Report bullying or inappropriate messages immediately.

**5. Family Responsibilities:**

- Parents will set a good example by limiting personal screen time.
- Kids will follow agreed rules and communicate challenges.
- Everyone will participate in screen-free family activities.

**Consequences for Breaking the Contract:**
1st Violation: ___________________
2nd Violation: ___________________
3rd Violation: ___________________

**Signatures:**

👨‍👩‍👧‍👦 Family Members:
____________________ (Parent/Guardian)
____________________ (Parent/Guardian)
____________________ (Child)
____________________ (Child)

📅 Date: ____________________

## 2. Technology Usage Log

**Why It Works:**
Tracking screen time helps identify patterns and address issues before they become habits.

**How to Use It:**
Use a simple log where family members record device use and reflect on how it makes them feel. This creates transparency and promotes self-awareness.

**Technology Usage Log Template**

**Purpose:** Use this log to track screen time, monitor device use, and reflect on its effects.

| Date | Device/Activity | Time Spent | Reason for Use | How I Felt After |
|---|---|---|---|---|
| 2024-12-01 | Homework on Laptop | 1 hour | School Project | Focused, Accomplished |
| 2024-12-02 | Social Media (Phone) | 2 hours | Leisure/Scrolling | Tired, Stressed |
| 2024-12-03 | Coding Game (Tablet) | 1.5 hours | Learning Activity | Motivated, Inspired |

**How to Use:**

1. **Fill it out daily:** Record device use, time spent, and its purpose (homework, gaming, social media).
2. **Reflect on emotions:** Note how screen time affected mood or energy.
3. **Review weekly:** Identify patterns and adjust screen rules accordingly.

**Why These Tools Work ?**

When parents have simple, effective tools in hand, they're better equipped to manage tech use with confidence. Practical templates eliminate guesswork, reduce daily tech-related stress, and create healthier digital habits that last. It's not just about giving advice, it's about making digital parenting easier, one actionable step at a time.

---

# Chapter 5: Encouraging Offline Engagement

Late one Friday afternoon, Karen glanced up from her phone to see her son, Max, sprawled out on the couch. The glow from his tablet illuminated his face, while the muffled sounds of a game buzzed in the background. "*Hey, Max,*" Karen said, "*want to go toss a ball outside?*" He barely looked up. "*Nah, I'm good.*" Karen felt a pang of worry, when did screen time become the default, and how could she help her kid rediscover the joys of life away from a screen?

This isn't just Karen's story; it's the story of countless families navigating the balance between online and offline worlds. Technology is woven into our daily routines, but as parents, we know there's so much value in unplugged moments. Encouraging offline engagement isn't about shunning devices, it's about making space for connection, creativity, and growth in ways that feel natural and exciting.

**The Case for Offline Activities**

The digital world offers endless entertainment, but it also comes with limits. Physical play, hands-on creativity, and face-to-face interactions build skills that no app can replicate. Research has shown that offline activities enhance problem-solving, boost emotional intelligence, and foster resilience.

For example, children who engage in outdoor play develop better motor skills and stronger social bonds than their screen-dependent peers. Board games teach collaboration and strategic thinking. Even mundane activities like cooking together can spark curiosity and teach valuable life lessons.

### Bridging the Digital and Physical Worlds

Transitioning from screen time to offline activities can feel challenging, especially when technology is so captivating. But it's not about forcing a divide, it's about showing how both worlds can complement each other. A child who loves video games might enjoy designing their own board game. A teen fascinated by photography could explore film cameras or hands-on darkroom techniques.

### Building Momentum for Engagement

Parents can start small. A family movie night could lead to a DIY film-making project. A walk in the park might inspire gardening or birdwatching. Simple shifts open the door to experiences that feel fresh and rewarding.

Offline engagement is an invitation, to pause, to play, and to connect in meaningful ways that strengthen relationships and create lasting memories. With the right approach, it's not just a shift in habits; it's a return to the essence of childhood itself.

## 5.1: Inspiring Creativity Beyond Screens

On a quiet Saturday morning, nine-year-old Emma sat on the living room floor surrounded by scraps of paper, glue sticks, and a rainbow of markers. Her mission? To create a tiny city for her collection of toy animals. Towers crafted from cardboard cereal boxes stood proudly beside paper towel roll skyscrapers. Her mother, Lisa, watched from the kitchen, amazed by how Emma could lose herself in a world of her own creation, without a single screen in sight.

Emma's tiny city wasn't just a creative outlet; it was a testament to how children's imaginations thrive when given the tools and the space to explore. Yet, with the dominance of digital entertainment, fostering these moments of hands-on creativity takes intention.

### Why Creativity Beyond Screens Matters

Screens are undeniably engaging, but they often limit creativity to pre-programmed options. Offline creative activities, however, encourage children to experiment, problem-solve, and develop their own ideas from scratch. These experiences nurture critical thinking and originality, skills that serve children far beyond childhood.

Consider this: building a fort out of blankets or painting a self-portrait isn't just fun; it's a process that teaches resourcefulness and persistence. These activities allow kids to express themselves in ways that can't be achieved with a swipe or a click.

### Activity Ideas to Spark Creativity

Parents frequently wonder where to start when it comes to inspiring offline creativity. The good news? The possibilities are endless, and they don't have to involve elaborate setups or expensive materials.

**1. Art Projects:**

- **Abstract Painting**: Provide a canvas, some paint, and let kids explore colors and textures. It's not about creating something perfect, it's about the joy of expression.
- **Nature Collages**: A walk in the park can turn into an art session. Collect leaves, flowers, and small twigs to arrange into beautiful collages.
- **DIY Stamps**: Using potatoes or sponges, kids can carve shapes to create their own stamps for cards or posters.

**2. Building Activities:**

- **LEGO Challenges**: Instead of following instructions, challenge kids to build their dream house, a vehicle, or even a bridge that can hold weight.

- **Cardboard Creations**: From castles to spaceships, cardboard boxes can be transformed into almost anything with a little tape and imagination.
- **Marble Runs**: Using household items like paper tubes and plastic cups, kids can design intricate marble run tracks.

3. **Music and Performance:**

- **Homemade Instruments**: Create tambourines from paper plates or shakers from jars filled with rice.
- **Puppet Shows**: Kids can craft puppets out of socks or paper bags and put on a play.
- **Songwriting**: Encourage them to write their own songs, whether they're silly jingles or heartfelt ballads.

### Kids Thriving in Non-Digital Hobbies

Real-life examples often inspire us to take action. Across the country, countless children are discovering joy and fulfillment in hobbies that don't involve screens.

### Case Study: Liam, the Young Carpenter

Liam, a ten-year-old from Oregon, discovered woodworking during a summer spent with his grandfather. Together, they built birdhouses, a bookshelf, and even a simple chair. Not only did Liam develop a new skill, but he also gained confidence and a deeper bond with his grandfather. Today, Liam proudly gifts his creations to family and friends.

### Case Study: Maya, the Budding Gardener

Maya, an eight-year-old from Texas, turned a corner of her backyard into a vegetable garden. She started small, planting tomatoes and peppers in pots. Over time, her garden grew into a thriving patch that now includes herbs and flowers. Maya says that gardening makes her feel calm and proud, especially when she gets to share her harvest at family dinners.

### Case Study: Carlos, the Inventor

Carlos, a twelve-year-old from Florida, found his passion in tinkering with old electronics. With a toolbox and some online tutorials, he started taking apart broken gadgets to understand how they worked. Over time, he began creating his own devices, including a homemade Bluetooth speaker. Carlos's curiosity has sparked an interest in engineering, and he's now dreaming of a future career in tech design.

### How to Encourage Participation ?

One of the keys to inspiring creativity is giving children the freedom to explore without fear of making mistakes. Encourage them to try new things and remind them that it's okay if their projects don't turn out as planned. Often, the process is more valuable than the result.

Additionally, make creativity a family affair. Parents can join in on art projects or building activities, making these moments an opportunity for connection. When kids see their parents engaged, it reinforces the idea that offline creativity is both fun and important.

### Transitioning Away from Screens

Switching from digital entertainment to offline activities can feel like a challenge, especially if screens have become a regular part of your family's routine. Here are some practical tips to make the transition smoother:

1. **Set Boundaries:** Create specific times for screen-free activities, like an hour after school or during weekends.

2. **Provide Options**: Keep art supplies, building materials, or musical instruments easily accessible, so kids can dive in when inspiration strikes.

**3. Model Behavior**: Show your own interest in creative hobbies, whether it's sketching, knitting, or cooking.

### The Lifelong Impact of Creativity

Inspiring creativity beyond screens isn't just about keeping kids entertained, it's about equipping them with tools to navigate the world with curiosity and confidence. These hands-on experiences lay the groundwork for innovation and adaptability, qualities that will serve them well as they grow.

When children dive into non-digital hobbies, they discover more than just new skills, they uncover parts of themselves they didn't know existed. And for parents, witnessing that transformation is one of the greatest rewards.

## 5.2: Social Skills Without Screens

On a warm summer afternoon, a group of kids gathered at the neighborhood park. There were no phones in sight, just a soccer ball, some sidewalk chalk, and a lot of laughter. Eight-year-old Jake took charge, organizing a quick game. "You be goalie!" he shouted to his friend Mia, who eagerly stepped into position. Within minutes, they were a team, working together, sharing strategies, and learning how to celebrate victories or brush off defeats.

These moments are priceless. They not only strengthen bonds but also teach skills like communication, teamwork, and empathy. In today's digital-first world, fostering these face-to-face interactions is more important than ever.

### The Decline of Social Interaction in a Digital World

Digital devices have changed how kids interact. While online chats and multiplayer games offer some level of connection, they often lack the depth and nuance of in-person communication. Eye contact, tone of voice, and body language, the core elements of human interaction, are missing.

Without regular opportunities for face-to-face engagement, children may struggle to develop essential social skills. This is why creating spaces and opportunities for real-world interaction is so critical.

**Strategies for Encouraging Face-to-Face Interactions and Teamwork**

Parents and educators can play a huge role in helping children build these vital skills. Here are a few strategies to encourage meaningful, screen-free interactions:

**1. Organize Group Activities**

- **Sports and Games**: Whether it's a pickup basketball game or a relay race, sports naturally encourage teamwork and communication. Kids learn how to rely on each other and strategize as a group.
- **Board Game Nights**: Gather friends or family for a game night. Games like charades or cooperative board games promote teamwork and problem-solving.

**2. Encourage Collaborative Projects**

- **Community Service**: Volunteer opportunities, like cleaning up a park or organizing a food drive, teach kids to work toward a shared goal while contributing to their community.
- **DIY Projects**: Building a treehouse or creating a school play encourages kids to delegate tasks and support each other's efforts.

**3. Promote Team-Based Clubs**

- **Drama Clubs**: Acting in plays requires kids to collaborate, listen, and adapt to others on stage.
- **Science Teams**: Working on group experiments or entering robotics competitions fosters a sense of camaraderie and shared accomplishment.

### The Power of Unstructured Play

While organized activities are valuable, unstructured play is just as crucial for developing social skills. It allows kids to explore relationships and learn conflict resolution on their own terms.

### Case Study: The Backyard Adventure

Take 10-year-old Ella and her friends, who transformed a simple backyard into a pirate ship, complete with imaginary treasure and secret codes. With no adult guidance, they negotiated roles, invented storylines, and resolved disagreements when someone wanted to "*walk the plank*" too soon.

Unstructured play like this helps children:

- Practice compromise and negotiation.
- Develop leadership and decision-making skills.
- Build resilience by working through minor conflicts independently.

### The Role of Parents and Guardians

Creating an environment that supports social interactions doesn't have to be complicated. It starts with small, intentional steps:

1. **Limit Screen Time During Social Hours**: Encourage kids to put away devices during meals, playdates, or family gatherings.

2. **Model Behavior**: Kids learn by example. Show them how to engage in meaningful conversations and active listening.

3. **Provide Resources**: Offer tools like sports equipment, art supplies, or access to community programs that make socializing easier.

## Examples of Kids Thriving Through Social Play

**Real-life stories show how impactful these strategies can be.**

### Ava's Theater Journey

Nine-year-old Ava was shy and struggled to speak up in class. Her parents enrolled her in a local drama club, hoping she'd find her voice. Over time, Ava not only learned to act, but also developed the confidence to lead group activities and mentor younger kids. Today, she credits her theater experience with teaching her how to communicate and collaborate.

### Ethan's Soccer Squad

Ethan's parents noticed he spent most of his free time gaming. Wanting him to balance his interests, they signed him up for a soccer team. At first, he resisted, preferring the virtual world. But after a few practices, Ethan discovered the joy of teamwork, forming friendships and learning to appreciate the effort required to achieve shared goals.

### Lila's Neighborhood Initiative

Twelve-year-old Lila organized a weekly bike ride for the kids in her neighborhood. What started as a small group turned into a community event, teaching her leadership and giving her peers a chance to bond in a fun, screen-free way.

## Balancing Technology and Social Skills

It's unrealistic to eliminate screens entirely, nor is it necessary. Instead, the focus should be on finding a balance. Digital communication has its place, but it should complement, not replace, face-to-face interactions.

One way to achieve this is by setting specific times for offline activities, like "Tech-Free Tuesdays" or weekend hikes. These breaks from technology give kids a chance to practice social skills in real-life settings.

**The Long-Term Benefits**

Encouraging social skills without screens doesn't just prepare children for today; it sets them up for life. These experiences teach empathy, adaptability, and emotional intelligence, qualities that are invaluable in personal relationships and professional environments alike.

Through teamwork, kids learn the value of collaboration. Through play, they discover how to connect authentically with others. And through your guidance, they gain the confidence to navigate social situations with ease.

## 5.3: Making the Transition Easier

It was a rainy Saturday morning when Mia, a mother of three, decided to test her limits. Her kids had been glued to their tablets for hours, and she'd had enough. With a deep breath, she announced, "Alright, everyone, we're doing a screen-free weekend challenge!" Her declaration was met with groans and dramatic protests, but she stood firm, armed with an arsenal of activities. By Sunday evening, the house was buzzing with stories of their scavenger hunt, the pillow fort wars, and even a family cooking contest that ended with flour everywhere.

What Mia learned that weekend wasn't just how to keep her kids entertained without screens, it was the importance of shifting focus from what they were giving up to what they were gaining.

**Understanding the Resistance**

Reducing screen time isn't just about unplugging devices; it's about changing habits, and that's never easy. Kids, and even adults, often see screens as their go-to for entertainment, relaxation, and even social connection. So, when you introduce the idea of cutting back, it's natural to face pushback.

But resistance doesn't mean it's impossible. The key lies in making the process feel less like a punishment and more like an opportunity.

**Tips for Reducing Screen Time Without Battles**

**1. Start Small and Build Momentum**

Begin by introducing shorter, manageable screen-free periods. For instance, designate an hour after school as "tech-free time" for reading, drawing, or outdoor play. Once this becomes routine, gradually extend these periods.

**2. Involve Your Kids in the Decision-Making**

Children are more likely to embrace change when they feel included. Sit down with them and discuss why reducing screen time is important. Let them help create the new rules, like setting limits on screen use during meals or before bed.

**3. Create a Reward System**

Turn screen-free time into a game. For example, each hour spent without screens earns points that can be redeemed for a fun family outing or a small treat.

**4. Offer Engaging Alternatives**

The easiest way to reduce screen reliance is by offering equally appealing activities:

- Plan a backyard camping adventure.
- Organize a craft session with supplies for painting or model building.
- Encourage them to try cooking or baking with you.

**5. Lead by Example**

Kids mimic what they see. If you're constantly on your phone or laptop, they'll likely do the same. Model the behavior you want to see by putting your devices away during family time.

## Fun Challenges to Keep It Interesting

Making the transition fun rather than restrictive can work wonders. Here are some creative challenges that families can try:

**1. Screen-Free Weekends**

Set aside one weekend a month when everyone, parents included, goes without screens. Fill the time with board games, outdoor activities, and family projects.

**Case Study: The Johnson's Screen-Free Adventure**

The Johnson family decided to go screen-free one weekend every month. On their first attempt, they discovered a nearby hiking trail and spent hours exploring, collecting leaves, and spotting wildlife. By the end of the weekend, they were exhausted but happier, with memories they still talk about today.

**2. "Analog Hour" Every Evening**

Pick an hour each evening where no one uses screens. Instead, encourage activities like storytelling, playing instruments, or working on a puzzle together.

**3. Creative Contests**

Challenge your kids to design and build something from scratch, like a cardboard castle or a LEGO city. Offer small prizes to make it even more exciting.

## The Role of Routine in Easing the Transition

Structure is your best friend when reducing screen time. Establishing clear routines helps kids know what to expect and makes the absence of screens feel normal rather than punitive.

**Morning Routines**: Start the day with offline activities, like stretching, journaling, or a quick family walk.

**Evening Routines**: Replace pre-bedtime screen time with a calming activity, like reading or drawing.

When kids know there's a plan, they're less likely to complain or ask for their devices.

## Examples of Screen-Free Success

### Liam's Reading Revival

Liam, a 10-year-old who spent most of his free time gaming, rediscovered his love for books after his parents introduced a "no screens after dinner" rule. With nothing else to do, he picked up a fantasy novel that quickly became his favorite series. Within weeks, Liam was devouring books and even started writing his own stories.

### Sophia's New Hobby

When Sophia's parents limited her screen time, she turned to gardening. What started as a small patch of flowers soon became a thriving vegetable garden. Now, she spends her afternoons tending to her plants and learning about sustainability.

## Handling Pushback and Meltdowns

Not every child will embrace screen-free time without resistance. Here are some ways to navigate those rough moments:

- **Stay Calm**: Understand that frustration is a natural response to change.

- **Acknowledge Their Feelings**: Let them express their disappointment and show empathy, but remain firm about the limits.
- **Offer Comfort Activities**: Suggest comforting alternatives, like a favorite non-digital game or a family story session.

Consistency is key. Over time, even the most reluctant kids will adjust to the new norm.

**The Bigger Picture**

Reducing screen time isn't just about cutting back; it's about rediscovering the joys of offline life. From stronger family connections to newfound hobbies, the benefits are endless.

By framing the transition as an exciting challenge rather than a restriction, you can create positive associations with screen-free activities. And as your family learns to thrive without constant digital stimulation, you'll realize just how much richer life can be.

---

# Chapter 6: Special Considerations and Challenges

Raising children in today's world isn't a one-size-fits-all approach. Just as every child is unique, so too are the challenges and considerations that come with balancing their screen time and offline experiences. For some families, it's a matter of navigating the delicate dance between technology use and social interaction. For others, the struggle may be more intense; whether due to special needs, different learning styles, or simply the fast-paced nature of our digital world.

Take Olivia, for example. A single mother of two, she found herself overwhelmed when her son, Jake, began exhibiting behavioral challenges tied to excessive screen time. Despite trying to enforce limits, the constant battles left Olivia feeling drained. What she didn't realize at first was that Jake's need for structure and routine was far more critical than just limiting screens. As she adjusted her parenting approach, incorporating more patience and routine, she began to see a shift in his behavior. It was a reminder that sometimes, the biggest challenges lie not in the tools we use, but in how we adapt to the needs of our children.

But what about families facing even more complex situations? How do we address those who may be struggling with attention disorders, autism, or other conditions that require a more tailored approach to technology use? How do we ensure that all children, regardless of their unique needs, benefit from the strategies discussed, without feeling excluded or overwhelmed?

These are the kinds of questions that often arise when tackling the balance between technology and childhood. This chapter explores these deeper, often more complex issues, diving into special considerations and offering practical insights into overcoming some of the toughest challenges. From accommodating children with special needs to managing the influence of peer pressure and societal expectations, we'll uncover strategies for building a more balanced, healthy approach to parenting in the digital age.

Every family's journey is different, and finding the right balance is a continuous process. It's not about perfection, it's about progress and patience.

## 6.1: Screen Time for Children with Special Needs

One evening, Sarah, a mother of an 8-year-old boy named Max, sat at the kitchen table, scanning through her emails. Max, who has autism, sat beside her, absorbed in a tablet. Sarah's mind raced as she glanced at the clock, knowing that her son had been on his device for over two hours now. She had heard so much about the dangers of excessive screen time, but she also knew that Max was more engaged with his tablet than anything else. The apps he used weren't just entertainment, they were tools that helped him communicate and learn.

It wasn't long ago that Sarah had been worried about Max's development in school. He struggled with social interactions, had trouble focusing, and found it difficult to express himself. But when she introduced speech therapy apps and interactive learning games, Max's progress was tangible. The challenge, however, was finding the right balance. Technology had become both a tool for progress and a potential pitfall. Where did she draw the line?

For parents like Sarah, balancing therapeutic tech use with recreational screen time can be a fine line. The truth is, technology can offer unparalleled support to children with special needs. Whether it's helping with communication, learning, or even social skills, screen time can be a vital part of their development. But how much is too much? And how do we ensure that screen time doesn't turn from a helpful tool into a distraction that hampers other areas of life?

### The Role of Technology in Supporting Learning and Communication

Technology can play a transformative role for children with special needs. For children on the autism spectrum, like Max, speech apps and educational games can open up new ways to communicate and learn. These tools, which often incorporate visuals, audio, and interactive elements, allow children to process information in ways that might be more accessible than traditional teaching methods.

A case in point is the use of apps designed for non-verbal children to communicate. Apps like **"Proloquo2Go"** are life-changing for kids who struggle with verbal expression. By using pictures, symbols, and phrases, these apps allow children to build sentences, making communication more natural and less frustrating. For many parents, these apps serve as a bridge between their child's thoughts and the outside world.

Another example is the use of educational video games that teach math, reading, or social skills. "**Endless Alphabet**", for instance, helps children with learning disabilities understand letters, sounds, and words by combining animation with fun, interactive games. These tools support children who might find traditional classroom settings overwhelming or difficult.

Yet, as effective as these technologies can be, they come with a responsibility to manage their use. It's easy for children to become absorbed in their devices, especially when they're engaging and rewarding. This is where the challenge for parents comes in: ensuring that screen time serves a functional purpose without overshadowing other important areas of their child's life.

## Balancing Therapeutic Tech Use and Recreational Screen Time

As we've seen with Max, technology can be both a helpful tool and a potential source of distraction. The key lies in striking the right balance. So, how can parents ensure their child's screen time is productive and not harmful?

First, it's important to differentiate between therapeutic screen time and recreational screen time. The former includes activities that directly support your child's development, such as using apps for speech therapy, cognitive exercises, or educational games. These activities are goal-oriented and should be seen as part of your child's learning or therapy routine. The latter refers to time spent on entertainment, like watching YouTube videos, playing video games, or browsing social media, activities that may not directly contribute to your child's development.

Experts suggest setting clear, structured limits on both types of screen time. For example, you could allocate a certain amount of time each day to therapeutic tech, followed by a scheduled break before engaging in recreational screen activities. This helps establish a healthy routine that prioritizes developmental goals while still allowing for downtime and relaxation.

## Case Study: Emma's Journey with Technology

Emma, a mother of a 10-year-old girl with ADHD, faced a unique set of challenges when it came to managing screen time. Emma's daughter, Sophie, was highly distractible and often found it difficult to focus on tasks, including homework. However, Sophie loved using her tablet for educational games that required her to solve puzzles and practice math. Emma quickly realized that these games had a positive impact on Sophie's ability to concentrate, but she also noticed that Sophie typically struggled to shift focus from the tablet to other activities.

Emma took a proactive approach to balancing Sophie's screen time. She set specific time slots for educational games in the morning, followed by a "**tech-free**" time after lunch. During this break, Sophie was encouraged to engage in physical activities like drawing, reading, or playing with her toys. Over time, Sophie became better at managing her attention. Emma also implemented a system of rewards, where Sophie could earn extra recreational screen time after completing non-tech activities like reading or doing a puzzle with her family.

Emma's experience highlights the importance of structure and consistency. By establishing a clear routine and making recreational screen time a reward rather than a default activity, she helped Sophie learn to balance both productive and leisure activities.

**Setting Boundaries: Practical Guidelines for Parents**

To effectively manage screen time for children with special needs, parents can benefit from a few practical strategies:

1. **Set clear time limits**: Whether it's therapeutic or recreational, establishing time limits is crucial. A common guideline is no more than one to two hours of recreational screen time per day, but this can vary depending on your child's age and needs. For therapeutic use, parents should consult with their child's therapist or teacher to determine how much screen time is beneficial for their child's development.

2. **Use screen time as a tool, not a crutch:** While technology can enhance learning, it should not replace human interaction or physical activities. Encourage your child to engage in activities like reading, outdoor play, or art projects as well. A well-rounded routine fosters cognitive, physical, and emotional development.

3. **Incorporate breaks**: Continuous screen time can lead to eye strain, restlessness, or overstimulation. Schedule regular breaks to

help your child reset, move around, and refocus. Breaks can be as simple as stretching, taking a walk, or doing an activity that doesn't involve screens.

**4. Be mindful of content**: Not all apps or games are created equal. Choose educational tools and games that align with your child's developmental needs. Many apps offer personalized settings that adjust to your child's learning pace, which can be especially helpful for children with special needs.

**5. Create a tech-free zone**: Designating certain areas of the home as tech-free zones can help maintain a healthy balance. The dinner table, bedrooms, or living rooms can be areas where devices are put away, allowing for face-to-face interaction and bonding time.

**6. Monitor usage**: Using parental control tools to track screen time and limit access to certain apps can be a helpful way to manage what your child is doing online. Many devices and apps offer parental settings that allow you to control access to content, making it easier to ensure your child is engaging in safe and appropriate activities.

### Finding the Right Approach for Your Child

Every child's needs are different, and there's no one-size-fits-all solution when it comes to screen time. Some children may thrive with more therapeutic technology, while others may require more structured breaks or limits on recreational screen use. It's essential to work closely with professionals, such as therapists, teachers, or pediatricians, to create a plan that suits your child's unique needs.

Remember that balance is key. Technology can be an incredible tool for learning and communication, but it should complement-not replace-other important aspects of your child's life. By setting clear boundaries, monitoring usage, and fostering a healthy relationship with screens, you can ensure that technology remains a positive force in your child's development.

## 6.2: Navigating Screen Time with Teens

One Friday night, Claire was scrolling through her phone in her room. Her parents were calling her for dinner, but the glow of her screen kept her glued to the spot. On her Instagram feed, it seemed like everyone was having the time of their lives, concerts, group hangouts, perfectly edited selfies. Claire felt a pang of loneliness, even though just an hour earlier, she

had been joking around with her family downstairs.It wasn't that she wanted to be at the concert or out with friends; it was the feeling that everyone else seemed connected, while she wasn't.

Claire's parents, Mark and Lisa, didn't quite know how to approach the situation. They recognized that social media and screen time had become integral to Claire's social life, but they also saw how it sometimes left her anxious or distant. Like many parents of teens, they wondered: how do you help a teenager balance independence and responsibility in a world dominated by screens?

### Fostering Independence and Responsibility

The teenage years are a pivotal time when kids begin carving out their identities, often leaning heavily on their peers for validation. Social media and screens become a significant part of this process, offering both a platform for expression and a source of constant comparison. The goal for parents isn't to cut off their teen's access to these tools entirely, it's to guide them in using them responsibly.

**Start with open conversations**. It's easy to jump into rule-setting, but establishing trust begins with understanding. Ask questions like, "What do you enjoy about social media?" or "Do you ever feel stressed about keeping up with what's happening online?" These questions can open the door to meaningful discussions, making it easier to introduce limits without it feeling like a punishment.

For example, Claire's parents decided to approach her during a calm moment over the weekend. Instead of reprimanding her for not coming to dinner on time, they asked about the concert photos she had been looking at. This led to a candid discussion about how social media often amplifies FOMO, making it seem like everyone else is living a picture-perfect life.

**Create a shared plan**. Teens are far more likely to follow rules they've helped establish. Sit down together and draft a screen time plan that balances their need for connection with healthier boundaries. This could include agreed-upon times for device use, like no phones during meals or after a certain hour at night. By involving your teen in the process, you're empowering them to take responsibility for their choices.

### Managing Social Media Use

Social media is a double-edged sword. It can foster creativity, friendships, and self-expression, but it can also heighten insecurities, breed comparison, and exacerbate FOMO. Helping teens navigate these platforms requires both proactive strategies and ongoing support.

**Encourage mindful usage**. Teach your teen to be intentional about their social media use. This could mean curating their feeds to include more positive, inspiring content or setting aside specific times for scrolling rather than mindlessly opening apps throughout the day. For instance, Claire decided to follow more accounts focused on her interests, like photography and travel, instead of influencers whose posts left her feeling inadequate.

**Set limits on apps**. Many social media platforms now have built-in tools to track and limit time spent on the app. Work with your teen to set reasonable daily limits, perhaps 30 minutes to an hour for each platform. This helps them stay connected without falling into the rabbit hole of endless scrolling.

**Address the comparison trap**. Social media thrives on highlight reels, but it's important to remind teens that what they see online isn't the full story. Share examples from your own life of moments that might look perfect on the outside but were far from it in reality. Over time, this helps teens build a healthier perspective on what they see online.

### Tackling FOMO

The fear of missing out is a powerful driver of screen time, especially for teens. It's the nagging feeling that something amazing is happening without them, and social media has a way of amplifying this anxiety. Addressing FOMO requires both practical strategies and emotional support.

**Encourage offline connections**. One of the best ways to combat FOMO is by helping your teen create meaningful in-person experiences. Whether it's organizing a family game night, encouraging them to join a sports team, or supporting their hobbies, these activities can provide a sense of fulfillment that isn't tied to screens.

For example, Claire's parents started hosting "Friday unplugged nights," where the whole family put their phones away and spent the evening baking, playing board games, or watching a movie together. At first, Claire was resistant, but over time, she began to look forward to these moments of connection.

**Introduce digital detox challenges**. Making it a game can make reducing screen time more appealing. Suggest fun challenges like a "screen-free weekend" or "phone-free dinners." You can even make it a family effort, where everyone participates and shares how it impacts their mood or stress levels.

**Build confidence in their choices**. FOMO often stems from feeling uncertain about their own decisions. Help your teen understand that it's okay to miss out on some things and that their worth isn't tied to being involved in everything. This mindset takes time to develop, but consistent encouragement can make a big difference.

**Case Study: Jake's Journey with Social Media**

Jake, a 16-year-old with a passion for music, found himself increasingly drawn to TikTok. He loved sharing clips of his guitar covers and connecting with other young musicians, but he also noticed that he felt drained after spending hours scrolling through other users' posts. The constant comparisons made him question his talent, and he started avoiding opportunities to perform live, fearing he wasn't good enough.

Jake's parents noticed his change in behavior and decided to step in. Instead of banning TikTok outright, they encouraged him to use it in a way that aligned with his goals. They suggested he limit his time on the app to an hour a day and focus on creating content rather than consuming it. They also signed him up for a local music workshop, where he could meet other teens who shared his passion.

Over time, Jake's confidence grew. He still used TikTok, but in a way that felt empowering rather than overwhelming. The mix of online and offline interactions helped him feel more balanced and less consumed by FOMO.

**Transitioning to Healthier Habits**

Shifting screen habits doesn't happen overnight, especially for teens who are deeply entrenched in their digital lives. It requires patience, consistency, and a willingness to adapt as you go.

**Be a role model**. Teens are more likely to follow your lead than your words. If you're constantly checking your phone during conversations or scrolling through social media late at night, it's hard to enforce boundaries with your teen. Show them that you value balance by practicing it yourself.

**Celebrate progress**. Acknowledge and praise your teen when they make positive changes, no matter how small. Whether it's cutting down their screen time by 10 minutes a day or choosing to spend an afternoon offline, these moments deserve recognition.

**Keep the dialogue open.** Navigating screen time is an ongoing process. Check in regularly with your teen to see what's working, what's challenging, and how you can support them.

By addressing independence and responsibility, managing social media use, and tackling FOMO, parents can help their teens build healthier relationships with their screens. The goal isn't perfection, it's progress. And with the right strategies, it's possible to create a balance that empowers teens to thrive both online and offline.

## 6.3: Cultural and Individual Differences

One evening in a bustling kitchen in Delhi, Meera was preparing dinner while her two children, Aryan and Kavya, sat nearby. Aryan was engrossed in a math app on his tablet, while Kavya scrolled through her Instagram feed. Meera glanced at them and sighed softly. She had grown up in a home where evenings were spent sharing stories, playing games, or helping in the kitchen. Technology had changed things, both enriching and complicating family dynamics.

Meera's story reflects a global reality. Across the world, families navigate tech use in ways rooted in cultural values, traditions, and individual beliefs. Understanding these differences helps parents create tech rules that align with what matters most to them.

### The Role of Family Values in Tech Use

Every family has core values influenced by cultural norms, traditions, and personal beliefs. These values shape how parents set tech rules, whether they see technology as a learning tool, a source of entertainment, or a potential disruption.

**Examples of Culturally-Informed Tech Rules**:

1. **Education-Driven Approach**:
   - In **South Korea**, where education is highly valued, the Lee family limits tech use to academic purposes. Their son Ji-hoon follows strict screen-time rules, using his tablet primarily for schoolwork and online courses. Though he sometimes feels left out when friends discuss popular video games, he excels academically, a trade-off his family accepts.
2. **Balance-Oriented Approach:**
   - In **San Antonio, Texas**, the Martinez family enjoys blending learning and leisure. Technology brings them together through family movie nights and online games. Their rules are relaxed but balanced with outdoor play, weekend barbecues, and board game nights.

**Cultural Practices and Tech Boundaries**

Cultural traditions strongly influence how tech is perceived. In some households, shared family activities take priority over individual screen time, while others encourage personal digital exploration.

**Contrasting Cultural Practices:**

- **Mediterranean Mealtime Tradition:**
  - In many Mediterranean countries, family meals are sacred. Phones are banned from the dinner table as a rule, emphasizing meaningful conversations. Maria, a mother of three in Athens, enforces this policy: "*Dinner is the one time we're all together. We share stories, not screens*."

- **Individualized Tech Exploration**:
    - In some **Western cultures**, individual tech use is encouraged to support hobbies and online learning. Tech rules are customized for each child's needs, reflecting a culture that values independence.

**Key Insight**:

Even within the same culture, tech rules can differ based on personal beliefs, family schedules, and access to technology.

**Balancing Cultural Norms with Modern Challenges**

Globalization and technological advancement have reshaped how families blend cultural traditions with modern realities. Consider the Patel family, who moved from Mumbai to Toronto. In India, their children were used to minimal screen time under their grandparents' supervision, playing traditional games after school. After moving to Canada, with both parents working long hours, screens became essential for learning and entertainment.

The Patels initially felt guilty about this shift but adapted by integrating cultural traditions into their new routine. They started **hosting family nights** featuring traditional Indian board games and Bollywood movie marathons, blending familiar customs with modern entertainment.

**Recognizing Individual Differences Within Families**

Cultural values set the stage, but each child responds differently to technology. What works for one may be ineffective for another, even in the same family.

**Example: Tailoring Tech Rules**

Siblings Emma and Jake couldn't be more different:

- **Emma**, a bookworm, only uses her tablet for reading and school projects.

- **Jake**, a tech enthusiast, loves gaming and spends hours chatting with friends online.

Their parents, the Thompsons, initially enforced the same screen-time rules for both kids, but this led to frustration. Eventually, they customized their approach: Emma got more time on educational apps, while Jake balanced gaming with outdoor activities. This personalized strategy reduced conflict while supporting each child's unique needs.

**Bridging Generational Gaps**

Many families face a digital generation gap. For grandparents who grew up without smartphones or social media, tech can seem intrusive, while younger generations see it as essential. Misunderstandings often arise when tech habits clash with traditional family values.

**Example: Finding Middle Ground**

In the Nguyen household, where three generations live under one roof, tech rules sparked family debates. The grandparents wanted a complete screen ban during family gatherings, while the parents saw devices as tools for sharing family photos and playing music. After a thoughtful family meeting, they agreed on a compromise: *Phones were allowed only for sharing content, not for scrolling social media.* This solution respected the grandparents' desire for connection while acknowledging the teens' digital habits.

**Practical Guidelines for Managing Cultural and Individual Tech Use**

1. **Define Core Values**:

   - Discuss as a family what matters most, whether it's education, connection, creativity, or mindfulness. Use these values to guide tech rules.

2. **Blend Old and New Traditions**:

- Incorporate cultural customs into tech-free family time. For example, if storytelling is a family tradition, create **digital storybooks** together or record oral histories.

3. **Stay Flexible:**

- Be willing to adjust tech rules as children grow and their needs change. What works for a six-year-old may need rethinking for a teenager.

4. **Encourage Balance:**

- Promote **screen-free hobbies**, sports, cultural activities, and creative projects that build meaningful offline experiences.

5. **Keep the Dialogue Open**:

- Schedule **family check-ins** to adjust rules, share concerns, and make sure everyone feels heard and respected.

**Final Thought: The Power of Personalization**

There's no universal formula for managing screen time, it's about what works best for each family. By understanding how cultural beliefs, family values, and individual differences shape tech use, families can create **customized digital strategies** that honor their heritage while embracing modern possibilities. With **open communication**, and **shared responsibility**, technology can enhance, not replace, the meaningful connections that matter most.

While every family faces screen-time challenges, cultural backgrounds and financial realities add unique layers to digital parenting. To create an inclusive tech environment, we must understand how these factors shape screen habits and explore practical solutions that fit all households.

## 6.4: Socioeconomic and Cultural Inclusivity: Bridging the Digital Divide

Digital parenting is far from a one-size-fits-all experience. Cultural traditions, socioeconomic realities, and access to technology shape how families engage with the digital world. Some families embrace technology as a path to educational success, while others struggle with limited internet access or cultural concerns about its influence on personal values.

To support parents from all walks of life, we must acknowledge these differences while offering **affordable, practical solutions** and **culturally sensitive strategies** that ensure every child benefits from the digital age.

**How Cultural Backgrounds Shape Tech Use ?**

Cultural values shape how parents view technology and its role in child development. What works in one family may conflict with the norms or beliefs of another. Understanding these dynamics helps create a respectful, culturally aware approach to digital parenting.

**Global Perspectives on Technology Use**

1. **Tech as a Learning Tool:**
   - **South Korea & Japan:** Tech-driven education is deeply integrated, with coding, robotics, and AI being taught from an early age. Screen time is often seen as an investment in future careers.
2. **Preserving Cultural Identity:**
   - **Indigenous and Rural Communities:** Some families limit screen time to preserve traditions, emphasizing oral storytelling, crafts, and nature-based activities over digital interactions.

**3. Social Connectedness vs. Privacy:**

- **Western Cultures:** Social media often promotes openness and personal branding.
- **Privacy-Centered Cultures:** In countries like Germany or Scandinavian nations, strict privacy laws reflect parental concerns about online surveillance and data sharing.

**Parenting Insight: Cultural Sensitivity in Tech Rules**

*"Think of your family's values when creating tech rules. Does your culture value face-to-face family time, community engagement, or academic success? Use these as guiding principles when setting boundaries."*

**Addressing Socioeconomic Barriers**

Access to technology can be limited by **financial constraints**, **geographic location**, or **technological literacy gaps**. Offering budget-friendly solutions helps level the playing field and ensures digital literacy for all families.

**Budget-Friendly Tech Strategies**

**1. Free or Low-Cost Tech Access:**

- **Public Libraries:** Many libraries loan tablets, laptops, and Wi-Fi hotspots for free.
- **School Tech Programs:** Many schools provide tech equipment through grants or donation programs.

**Examples:**

- In the U.S., **Google's Chromebook Program** provides discounted devices to underfunded schools.
- In the U.K., **BBC Micro:bit** distributes free coding devices to students.

**2. Open Educational Resources (OERs):**
*Free, high-quality learning platforms accessible from any device.*

**Recommended Platforms:**

- **Khan Academy:** Free online courses for all ages.
- **Code.org:** Learn coding and computer science.
- **Duolingo:** Free language learning.
- **Coursera (Audit Mode):** University-level courses for free (certificate optional).

**3. Device Discounts & Donations:**

- **Nonprofits Offering Tech Support:**
    - **PCs for People (U.S.):** Low-cost devices for low-income families.
    - **EveryoneOn:** Free or discounted internet and devices for eligible families.
    - **World Computer Exchange:** Internationally distributes refurbished devices to underserved communities.
- **Tech Stores & Retailers:**
    - **Amazon Renewed:** Certified refurbished devices.
    - **Microsoft Refurbished PCs:** Affordable laptops for home learning.
    - **Local Tech Drives:** Participate in community tech donation events.

**4. Internet Access Assistance:**

Many governments and private companies offer subsidized internet access for families in need.

**Examples:**

- **Lifeline (U.S.):** Discounted phone and internet services for low-income households.

- **Internet Essentials (Comcast):** Low-cost internet for qualifying families.

**Practical Recommendations for Every Budget**

**1. Set Screen Time Rules That Don't Require Tech:**

- Use offline activity guides, printable worksheets, and books.

**2. Use Shared Devices Wisely:**

- Set time slots for school, social, and play activities.
- Use family calendars to manage device use fairly.

**3. Build a Local Support Network:**

- Join tech-sharing communities or swap programs at local community centers.
- Tap into parent-led Facebook groups offering device tips and free learning resources.

**Creating an Inclusive Tech Environment at Home**

1. **Inclusive Family Discussions:** Involve kids in setting screen time rules while acknowledging their unique learning needs.
2. **Tech-Free Traditions:** Honor family traditions by scheduling tech-free cultural activities, such as cooking traditional meals, storytelling nights, or community service.
3. **Respect for Privacy:** Teach children about privacy, especially in cultures where online visibility may be discouraged.

**Why Cultural and Socioeconomic Inclusivity Matters**

By understanding **cultural values**, **economic disparities**, and **access challenges**, we can create a more inclusive digital world. Every family deserves access to tools, support, and resources that empower them to thrive in today's digital environment, regardless of where they come from or what they can afford.

## 6.5: Teenagers and Social Media: Navigating the Digital Maze

For today's teens, social media is both a lifeline and a potential pitfall. It's where they connect, learn, and express themselves, but also where they face some of their biggest emotional and social challenges. Understanding social media's psychological impact helps parents support teens in creating a healthy digital balance while maintaining meaningful family relationships.

### The Psychological Impact of Social Media

Social media's influence goes beyond sharing selfies or funny memes. It has profound effects on teens' mental health, identity formation, and sense of self-worth.

**1. The Comparison Trap: When "Perfect" Becomes the Enemy**

**What It Is:**

Teens scroll through carefully curated photos and videos showcasing idealized lives. Seeing these filtered realities can create unrealistic expectations and lead to insecurity.

Example:

- **Sophia's Story:** Sophia, 15, compares herself to influencers on Instagram. Despite being a straight-A student, she often feels she's "not good enough" because her life seems boring compared to theirs. This constant comparison leaves her anxious and self-critical.

**How to Help**:

- **Media Literacy Talks:** Discuss how social media creates "highlight reels" and why comparing real life to curated content is unfair.
- **Practice Gratitude Journals:** Encourage teens to keep a journal listing three things they're grateful for daily. This helps shift focus from comparison to personal appreciation.
- **Follow Positive Influencers:** Help teens find creators promoting mental health, body positivity, or social activism.

**2. Social Validation and FOMO (Fear of Missing Out)**

**What It Is:**

Social validation through likes, comments, and shares can be addictive. Fear of Missing Out (FOMO) occurs when teens see peers attending events or having experiences they aren't part of, sparking loneliness and exclusion.

**Example**:

- **Alex's Experience:** Alex wasn't invited to a classmate's birthday party. Seeing Instagram stories of the party made him feel left out and isolated, even though he spent the evening with close family.

**How to Help**:

- **Mindful Posting Practice:** Teach teens to post for fun or creativity, not for validation.
- **Scheduled Social Media Use:** Limit social media check-ins to specific times of the day to reduce compulsive scrolling.
- **Offline Alternatives:** Organize family activities or allow teens to invite friends over to create memorable offline moments.

**3. Digital Addiction: Stuck in the Endless Scroll**

**What It Is:**

Social media platforms are designed to hook users through infinite scrolling, personalized feeds, and constant notifications. Teens can lose hours browsing content without realizing it.

**Example**:

- **Emma's Routine:** Emma spends hours scrolling TikTok before bed, often staying up until 2 AM despite her best intentions. She wakes up groggy and struggles to concentrate in class.

How to Help:

- **Use Screen Time Limits:** Set app time limits through phone settings or parental control tools.
- **Tech-Free Zones:** Declare areas like bedrooms or dinner tables tech-free to promote healthier habits.
- **Lead by Example:** Avoid scrolling during family time to model mindful tech use.

**Warning Signs of Social Media Overuse**

**Red Flags to Watch For:**

- **Mood Swings:** Increased irritability, anxiety, or sadness after using social media.
- **Sleep Problems:** Difficulty falling asleep due to nighttime scrolling.
- **Social Withdrawal:** Losing interest in offline activities or relationships.
- **Declining Grades:** Reduced focus or productivity in school.

## Additional Strategies for Creating Social Media Boundaries

### 1. Social Media Agreements: Clear Rules Everyone Understands

Create a **Family Social Media Agreement** with clear expectations, rules, and consequences. Involve teens in the process for shared accountability.

**What to Include:**

- Daily Screen Time Limits (e.g., 2 hours/day)
- Tech-Free Times (e.g., meals, before bed)
- Online Behavior Rules (e.g., respectful communication, privacy protection)

### 2. Teaching Critical Thinking & Digital Literacy

Help teens become **smart digital consumers** by teaching them how social media algorithms work and how content is curated.

**Tips for Developing Media Savvy Teens:**

- **Spot Fake Content:** Show how to identify misleading information, deepfakes, or clickbait.
- **Fact-Checking Tools:** Introduce websites like Snopes or FactCheck.org.
- **Discuss Algorithms:** Explain how algorithms push specific content to increase screen time.

### 3. Meaningful Online Engagement: Make Social Media Positive

Encourage teens to use social media **creatively** and **productively**, rather than just consuming content.

**Ideas for Positive Use:**

- **Start a Passion Project:** Launch a blog, YouTube channel, or TikTok page focused on something they love.
- **Join Online Communities:** Suggest joining learning platforms like Skillshare, Duolingo, or coding groups.
- **Follow Inspiring Accounts:** Look for influencers promoting causes like mental health, climate activism, or the arts.

**4. Emotional Check-Ins: Regularly Talk About Tech Use**

Have **weekly family check-ins** to discuss tech experiences. This keeps communication open and allows teens to express concerns about online pressure, bullying, or insecurity.

**Conversation Starters:**

- "What's the coolest thing you learned online this week?"
- "Have you ever seen something online that made you uncomfortable?"
- "Which accounts make you feel inspired or happy?"

**Case Study: Finding Social Media Balance**

**The Johnson Family Story:**

The Johnsons struggled when their daughter, Maya, became glued to her phone after starting high school. After noticing her declining grades and increased irritability, they held a family meeting. Together, they established screen-free zones, limited phone use after 8 PM, and encouraged Maya to join the school's art club. After a few months, Maya's mood improved, and she rediscovered her passion for painting, offline and online through an art-sharing page she created.

### Final Thought: A Digital World with Boundaries

Social media isn't the enemy, it's a tool. When used mindfully, it can inspire, educate, and connect. But left unchecked, it can harm teens' mental health, self-esteem, and social development.

By **staying involved**, **setting boundaries**, and **teaching digital literacy**, parents can help teens enjoy the **best of social media** while protecting their well-being. Balance isn't about banning, it's about building **smart, thoughtful habits** that empower teens to thrive in the digital age.

---

# Chapter 7: Weighing Benefits and Risks

When Clara handed her six-year-old son a tablet for the first time, she marveled at how quickly he navigated its interface. Within minutes, he was engrossed in a phonics app, pronouncing words with a surprising level of accuracy. Clara felt a wave of relief; maybe this could help him catch up with his peers in reading. But later that night, guilt crept in as she watched him swipe aimlessly through a cartoon channel. Was she helping him grow, or merely setting him on a path of dependency on screens?

This dilemma isn't unique to Clara. It's the internal tug-of-war every parent, educator, and policymaker faces when evaluating the role of technology in daily life. On one hand, the benefits are undeniable: access to global knowledge, tools that foster creativity, and platforms that connect families separated by miles. On the other hand, the risks loom large, addiction, reduced attention spans, and exposure to harmful content.

The question isn't whether technology is good or bad, it's far more nuanced than that. Understanding its impact requires peeling back the layers and analyzing both sides with care. Where does the promise of progress meet the point of caution? How do we ensure we're harnessing its strengths without falling prey to its pitfalls?

From the transformative power of digital tools to the unforeseen consequences of their misuse, this exploration dives into the heart of the balance. By unpacking real-world examples, expert insights, and actionable strategies, we'll uncover a framework for making informed decisions. This is a journey not of absolutes, but of finding equilibrium in a world driven by rapid technological change.

## 7.1: Positive Aspects of Technology

It all started with a simple question. Nine-year-old Ava sat at her kitchen table, flipping through a book on marine life. She looked up at her mom and asked, "Why can't we help clean the ocean?" It was an innocent curiosity, but it lit a spark. Her mother suggested they research ways to make an impact, and that's when Ava discovered a global initiative focused on ocean cleanup. Armed with her mom's tablet, Ava not only learned about the problem but also raised awareness through a video she created. Within weeks, her video had inspired her classmates to join her in organizing a local fundraiser, collecting enough money to sponsor a small cleanup project.

Ava's story is just one example of how technology, when used thoughtfully, can empower young minds to dream big and take action. Far from the bleak portrayals of tech's role in childhood, there's a brighter narrative to be told, one of connection, creativity, and opportunity.

**Access to Education**

One of technology's most transformative benefits lies in its ability to make education accessible to millions. No longer confined to classrooms, learning can now take place anywhere, at any time. Online platforms like Khan Academy, Duolingo, and Code.org provide free resources for students of all ages to learn math, languages, coding, and beyond.

Take the story of Samir, a 12-year-old boy from a rural village with no nearby schools. His parents saved up to buy a used smartphone, and with it, Samir gained access to an online math course. Within a year, he had mastered concepts far beyond his grade level and was mentoring other children in his community. Technology bridged the gap between his circumstances and his aspirations.

This democratization of knowledge is perhaps one of the greatest equalizers of our time. For children in underserved communities, a simple device can open doors to opportunities they never imagined.

## Building Connections Across Distances

The ability to connect with others, whether across the street or across the globe, has redefined relationships in the digital age. For families separated by long distances, video calls and messaging apps provide a way to stay involved in each other's lives. Kids can share their milestones with grandparents who live miles away, and cousins can play virtual games together despite being in different time zones.

Consider 14-year-old Mia, whose father was deployed overseas. Despite the physical distance, she used video chat to share her school projects, ask for advice, and even bake cookies while her dad watched from his phone. Technology helped maintain their bond, turning what could have been a lonely time into something deeply connected.

In addition to family ties, technology fosters friendships and collaborative efforts. Group projects no longer require everyone to meet in person. Tools like Google Docs and Zoom have made teamwork seamless, even when members are scattered. These connections teach kids valuable skills like collaboration, problem-solving, and cultural understanding.

## Sparking Creativity

If there's one area where technology truly shines, it's in its ability to ignite creativity. Kids now have access to tools that allow them to create art, compose music, write stories, and design games, all from the comfort of their homes. Platforms like Tinkercad and Scratch encourage children to think outside the box, blending learning with fun.

A 10-year-old named Ethan exemplifies this perfectly. Fascinated by animation, he started experimenting with free software on his family's computer. What began as simple stick figure drawings evolved into short films he shared with friends. His creations caught the attention of a local arts foundation, which offered him a scholarship for further training. Ethan's journey showcases how technology can turn hobbies into passions and passions into opportunities.

**Kids Using Tech for Good**

There's something incredibly inspiring about kids leveraging technology to make a difference. Stories like Ava's ocean cleanup initiative are becoming more common as young people use digital tools to amplify their voices. Social media platforms give kids a stage to advocate for causes they care about, whether it's raising money for a local animal shelter or spreading awareness about climate change.

Thirteen-year-old Maya started a blog to promote kindness in her school. Using a simple website builder, she shared tips on combating bullying and celebrated acts of kindness she observed around her. Her blog gained traction, leading to interviews with local newspapers and even an invitation to speak at a school assembly. Maya's experience proves that technology doesn't just give kids a voice, it gives them a megaphone.

**Striking a Balance**

Of course, the key to reaping these benefits lies in balance. Technology's positive impact isn't automatic; it requires guidance and intentionality. Parents and educators play a crucial role in steering kids toward constructive uses of tech. By introducing apps that encourage skill-building or suggesting projects that combine tech with real-world action, adults can help children see technology as a tool rather than a distraction.

Transitioning seamlessly between these benefits requires recognizing their interconnected nature. Education fuels creativity, creativity fosters connection, and connection inspires action. This cycle illustrates how technology, when approached with intention, can nurture a well-rounded generation equipped to tackle the challenges of tomorrow.

Whether it's helping a child access education, stay close to loved ones, or channel their creativity into meaningful projects, technology has the potential to uplift and inspire. It's a powerful reminder that even in an increasingly digital world, the heart of the matter lies in how we choose to use the tools at our disposal.

## 7.2: Signs of Overuse and What to Do

It was a quiet Saturday morning when Sarah noticed something unsettling. Her son, Lucas, had barely looked up from his tablet since breakfast. The usual spark in his eyes seemed dimmed, replaced by a vacant stare. When she asked him to help set the table for lunch, he barely registered her words, mumbling something about "one more level." This wasn't the first time, but it was the moment Sarah realized something had to change.

The signs had been there all along, difficulty focusing on tasks, irritability when the tablet was taken away, and a growing disinterest in activities he once loved. It dawned on her that what started as a harmless way to keep Lucas entertained had slowly turned into a dependency.

**Recognizing the Warning Signs**

In today's digital world, distinguishing between normal tech use and overuse can be tricky. Yet, there are telltale signs that screen dependency might be taking hold.

**1. Loss of Interest in Offline Activities**

Children who once loved drawing, playing sports, or building with blocks might show less enthusiasm for these activities, preferring screen time instead. A shift away from hobbies can indicate that screens are becoming the primary source of enjoyment.

**2. Mood Swings and Irritability**

Does your child get upset or frustrated when asked to put the device down? Sudden outbursts or emotional instability after tech interruptions can signal an unhealthy attachment.

**3. Physical Symptoms**

Complaints of headaches, eye strain, or sleep disruptions often accompany prolonged screen use. Watch for signs like squinting, rubbing the eyes, or struggling to fall asleep after evening screen sessions.

**4. Declining Academic or Social Performance**

Overuse can also affect schoolwork and relationships. Falling grades, missing deadlines, or avoiding friends might suggest that technology is taking precedence over responsibilities and connections.

**5. Secretive Behavior Around Screens**

If your child hides their device when you walk in or denies how much time they're spending on it, they might be aware of their overuse but unsure how to manage it.

## The Impact of Screen Dependency

Overuse of technology isn't just a matter of too much screen time, it can affect mental, emotional, and physical well-being. Excessive screen use has been linked to higher rates of anxiety, depression, and attention issues in children and teens. Social skills can also take a hit when face-to-face interactions are replaced by virtual ones.

For families, this dynamic can lead to tension, misunderstandings, and frustration. Parents may feel they're constantly nagging, while kids perceive rules as punitive rather than protective. The good news? With the right approach, it's possible to break the cycle and reset tech use in a way that benefits everyone.

### A Step-by-Step Action Plan to Reset Tech Use

#### Step 1: Reflect and Observe

The first step is understanding the extent of the problem. For a week, track your family's screen habits. How much time is spent on devices? What types of activities dominate, gaming, social media, educational content? Observing patterns can help pinpoint areas for improvement.

Sarah, for example, noticed Lucas spent nearly four hours a day on his tablet, with most of that time devoted to games. She also realized his usage spiked after school when he felt tired and unmotivated to do homework.

#### Step 2: Start a Family Conversation

Once you've gathered insights, sit down as a family to discuss the findings. Frame the conversation positively, emphasizing that the goal is to create healthier habits together, not to place blame.

Sarah approached Lucas by sharing her observations: "*I've noticed you're spending a lot of time on your tablet lately, and I want to make sure you're feeling your best. Let's talk about how we can balance things.*"

This approach invites collaboration and helps kids feel heard, reducing resistance to change.

**Step 3: Set Clear, Realistic Boundaries**

Work together to establish guidelines for tech use. These might include:

- Time limits: Set daily or weekly screen time caps based on age and needs.
- Tech-free zones: Designate areas like the dining room or bedrooms as screen-free.
- Scheduled breaks: Encourage 20-30 minutes of device-free time every hour to rest eyes and recharge.

For Lucas, the family agreed on no screens during meals and a two-hour limit after school, with part of that time dedicated to educational apps.

**Step 4: Replace Screens with Engaging Alternatives**

Simply reducing screen time isn't enough, kids need enjoyable alternatives to fill the void. Encourage outdoor play, board games, or creative projects that spark interest.

Sarah introduced Lucas to gardening, a hobby he quickly took to. Digging in the dirt and watching plants grow became a rewarding way for him to spend time offline.

**Step 5: Lead by Example**

Kids often mirror their parents' behavior. If adults in the household are glued to their phones, children will follow suit. Commit to mindful tech use as a family, showing that balance is a shared goal.

Sarah made a point to put her phone away during family time, demonstrating that she was just as invested in the reset.

### Step 6: Use Tech to Support, Not Replace

Technology itself isn't the enemy, it's how we use it. Introduce apps and platforms that encourage learning, creativity, and connection. For instance, instead of aimless scrolling, explore educational games or virtual museum tours together.

### Step 7: Monitor Progress and Celebrate Wins

Change doesn't happen overnight. Regularly check in as a family to assess how the new habits are working. Celebrate small successes, like sticking to time limits or rediscovering an old hobby.

Lucas's mood improved within weeks, and Sarah noticed he was sleeping better and engaging more during family activities. Recognizing these shifts helped the family stay motivated to maintain their new routine.

### Moving Toward Balance

Addressing screen overuse isn't about eliminating technology altogether, it's about restoring harmony. By setting boundaries, fostering open communication, and offering alternatives, families can ensure that tech enhances rather than detracts from their lives.

## 7.3: Digital Citizenship

It was during a family dinner when ten-year-old Mia shared her latest school project: creating a blog. Excitedly, she described how she posted her first article about her favorite books and received encouraging comments from classmates and strangers alike. But then her voice dropped. "Someone wrote something mean," she muttered, eyes cast downward.

Her mom leaned in, concerned. "*What did they say*?"

"*It's not important*," Mia shrugged, but her face told a different story. That evening, they discussed the concept of being a good digital citizen, someone who not only uses technology responsibly but also treats others with respect online. It was a pivotal moment that sparked the beginning of Mia's understanding of online etiquette, responsibility, and the impact of her digital actions.

**Building the Foundation of Digital Citizenship**

In an age where children navigate the digital world almost as often as the physical one, teaching them to be responsible, kind, and critical thinkers online has become essential. Digital citizenship is about empowering kids to use the internet thoughtfully, ensuring their actions contribute positively to the virtual community.

**1. Online Etiquette: More Than Just Manners**

Good manners don't stop at the dinner table—they extend to online interactions. Teaching kids about online etiquette means helping them recognize that words typed on a screen carry as much weight as words spoken aloud.

- **The Golden Rule of the Internet**

  Encourage children to treat others online the way they'd like to be treated. This simple guideline helps prevent bullying and promotes kindness. For instance, Mia's family worked together to craft thoughtful replies to comments on her blog, showing her how to model positive interactions.

- **Understanding Tone and Context**

  Online messages lack facial expressions and vocal tone, making misunderstandings easy. Role-playing scenarios can help kids grasp how their words might be interpreted. For example, saying

"That's not funny" might come across as harsh in text but playful in person.

- **Respecting Differences**

  The internet connects people from diverse backgrounds and beliefs. Teach kids to approach differing opinions with curiosity and respect rather than hostility. This creates opportunities for growth and learning instead of conflict.

## 2. Responsibility in the Digital World

Responsibility in the online sphere goes beyond personal behavior, it's also about understanding the consequences of one's digital actions.

- **The Digital Footprint: A Lasting Legacy**

  Everything posted online leaves a trail. Kids often underestimate how their comments, photos, and videos could resurface years later. Share real-life examples of people whose old social media posts impacted their future opportunities to drive this point home.

  One notable case involved a teenager who shared inappropriate jokes online, only to have them resurface during a college application process. Helping children understand the permanence of their online actions encourages them to think twice before posting.

- **Handling Peer Pressure Online**

  The internet can amplify peer pressure, especially on social media platforms where trends and challenges spread quickly. Discuss scenarios where kids might feel pressured to participate in viral challenges or share personal details and brainstorm strategies to say no.

- **Balancing Sharing and Privacy**

  Kids often don't realize the risks of oversharing online. Teach them to think critically about what information is safe to share and what should remain private. Use real-world analogies, like locking a diary or keeping a home address confidential, to make the concept relatable.

### 3. Encouraging Critical Thinking Online

The internet is a sea of information, but not all of it is reliable or safe. Teaching kids to evaluate content critically equips them to make informed decisions.

- **Spotting Fake News and Misinformation**

  Misinformation spreads easily, and kids are particularly susceptible to believing what they see online. Introduce activities that involve comparing credible news sources with fake articles to sharpen their discernment.

  For example, a teacher once assigned students to verify a viral story about a celebrity adopting a tiger. By researching reputable sources, the students learned the story was a hoax, sparking conversations about credibility.

- **Evaluating Sources**

  Teach kids to ask questions like: Who created this content? What's their motive? Are there other reliable sources confirming this information? These habits can help them navigate online spaces with confidence.

- **Recognizing Advertising Tactics**

  Many websites and apps target kids with ads disguised as content. Help children identify these tactics by discussing phrases like "sponsored" or "promoted" and explaining why companies use them.

## Activities to Foster Digital Citizenship

Learning about digital citizenship doesn't have to be dull. Engaging activities can make lessons stick while empowering kids to apply them in real-life scenarios.

### 1. The Digital Footprint Challenge

Ask children to search their name online and see what comes up. This activity can be an eye-opener, showing them the reach of their online presence. Follow up with a discussion about ways to protect their digital footprint, like using strong passwords and being selective about what they post.

### 2. Role-Playing Scenarios

Create situations where kids must decide how to respond to online dilemmas, such as:

- A friend shares a mean meme about another classmate.
- A stranger asks for personal details in a game chat.
- A popular influencer promotes a product that seems too good to be true.

Let them brainstorm responses and discuss the potential outcomes of each choice.

### 3. Fact-Checking Challenges

Turn critical thinking into a game by giving kids a mix of true and fake headlines. Task them with verifying which are accurate using reputable sources. This activity builds their research skills while demonstrating the importance of not taking everything at face value.

### 4. Creating a Digital Etiquette Guide

Have kids design a poster or infographic with their top tips for online etiquette. Displaying their work at home or school reinforces their learning and serves as a reminder to others.

### Transitioning from Knowledge to Action

Teaching digital citizenship isn't a one-time conversation, it's an ongoing process that evolves as kids grow and technology changes. By equipping them with the tools to navigate the digital world responsibly, we prepare them to use technology as a force for good.

Through discussions, activities, and real-life examples, kids can learn that their online actions matter, not just in the moment but for years to come. Empowering them to be thoughtful, respectful, and informed digital citizens ensures they're ready to thrive in a connected world.

## 7.4: Positive Technology Use: Unlocking Potential in the Digital Age

Conversations about screen time often focus on limits, risks, and dangers, and for good reason. But technology isn't just a challenge to manage, it's also a powerful tool for learning, creativity, and connection. By embracing its positive potential, parents can move beyond fear-based restrictions and help their children thrive in a connected world.

Let's explore how technology can enhance children's lives when used thoughtfully, through real-life examples and practical strategies that empower families.

### 1. Technology as a Tool for Learning

The right digital tools can open the door to endless learning opportunities. From mastering new languages to developing STEM skills, educational technology has transformed how children learn and grow.

**Inspiring Story**:

**Ella's Science Adventure**

Ella, a curious 10-year-old, developed a love for science through platforms like **National Geographic Kids and Scratch**, where she creates her own interactive games. One summer, she entered an online science competition, designing a project about ocean conservation, and she won! Her parents credit her screen time with sparking a lifelong passion for environmental advocacy.

**Practical Tips**:

- **Choose the Right Platforms**: Look for educational apps backed by experts, such as Khan Academy Kids, Duolingo, and Tynker.
- **Set Learning Goals**: Turn screen time into skill-building time by encouraging children to complete online courses or participate in creative challenges.
- **Explore Together**: Make learning a family activity. Watch nature documentaries or follow how-to tutorials on DIY projects.

**2. Technology as a Creative Outlet**

Digital tools unlock creativity like never before, allowing children to express themselves through art, music, filmmaking, and storytelling.

**Inspiring Story**:

**Leo the Filmmaker**

Leo, 14, turned his love of filmmaking into a passion project. Using his smartphone and free editing apps like **iMovie** and **Canva**, he created short films about everyday life in his neighborhood. His YouTube channel gained followers, and he even won an award at a local film festival. His screen time didn't just entertain him, it built skills that could shape his future career.

**Practical Tips:**

- **Explore Digital Art Platforms**: Apps like **Procreate**, **Canva**, or **GarageBand** let kids design, create music, and edit videos.
- **Start a Family Project**: Collaborate on creating a family photo album or a digital travel diary.
- **Share Their Work**: Encourage kids to share their creations in safe, supportive online communities like **ArtStation** or **DeviantArt**.

### 3. Technology as a Career Builder: Preparing for the Future

**Why It Matters**:

Digital literacy is no longer optional, it's essential for future careers. Technology opens doors to coding, design, marketing, and even entrepreneurship.

**Inspiring Story**:

**Liam's Coding Journey**

Liam, 13, loved playing video games but struggled with math in school. His parents signed him up for a **coding boot camp** through **Code.org**. Soon, Liam was designing simple games himself, blending fun with skill development. By the time he turned 16, he'd launched a mobile app to help younger kids learn math. His app gained 5,000 downloads within its first year, turning his hobby into a potential career.

**Practical Tips:**

- **Encourage Tech-Focused Hobbies**: Look into platforms like **Scratch, Tynker**, or **Codeacademy**.
- **Support Early Entrepreneurship**: Kids can start small businesses through platforms like **Etsy, Shopify**, or even **YouTube channels**.
- **Tech Competitions & Hackathons**: Sign them up for **STEM contests** or **robotics tournaments** for hands-on experience.

### 4. Technology as a Tool for Connection

Technology allows families to stay connected across distances and build communities with others who share similar interests or challenges.

**Inspiring Story:**

**The Patel Family's Global Connections**

After moving from India to Canada, the Patel family used technology to stay connected with their grandparents back home. Weekly **video calls** turned into storytelling nights, where the grandparents shared traditional folk tales. What began as a way to bridge the distance evolved into a cherished family tradition.

**Practical Tips**:

- **Schedule Virtual Meet-Ups**: Use video apps like **Zoom** or **WhatsApp** to stay connected with distant relatives.
- **Join Online Communities**: Encourage kids to join safe, monitored communities where they can discuss shared interests, from coding to climate activism.
- **Create Shared Experiences**: Host virtual family game nights or attend online events together.

### 5. Technology as a Platform for Social Impact

Technology empowers children to make a difference by raising awareness, organizing fundraisers, or volunteering virtually.

**Inspiring Story:**

**Lily the Climate Advocate**

At just 12 years old, Lily started an Instagram page dedicated to climate activism. She used her platform to organize virtual clean-up challenges and raise money for environmental charities. Her posts gained the attention of local news outlets, and she was invited to speak at a youth conference.

**Practical Tips**:

- **Get Involved**: Help children find online causes that resonate with them through platforms like **Change.org** or **GoFundMe**.
- **Teach Digital Advocacy**: Show them how to spread awareness by creating petitions or sharing educational videos.
- **Start Small:** Even simple projects like organizing a local charity event can build tech and leadership skills.

**Why Emphasizing Positive Tech Use Matters ?**

**Shifting the Narrative**:

By focusing on potential instead of restrictions, parents can create an atmosphere where technology is seen as an **opportunity** rather than a threat. It's not about **screen time limits alone**, it's about **screen time purpose**. When used mindfully, technology becomes a bridge to learning, creativity, and personal growth.

**Empower, Don't Fear:**

Instead of fearing the digital world, empower your children to explore its possibilities with the right guidance, clear boundaries, and consistent support. Technology isn't the enemy, it's a tool. How we use it determines its value.

---

# Conclusion: The Path to Lifelong Digital Wellness

One evening, as the Smith family sat together scrolling through their devices, a moment of quiet reflection broke the usual routine. Mrs. Smith suggested a simple idea, setting aside one evening a week as "tech-free family night." The kids groaned, and Mr. Smith hesitated, but they decided to give it a shot. By the end of their first board game night, laughter replaced notifications, and the kids didn't even ask for their phones. This small change ignited a journey toward digital balance and connection, proving that even tiny steps can lead to meaningful transformations.

This story illustrates a powerful truth: achieving lifelong digital wellness isn't about drastic overhauls but about intentional choices, one step at a time. Let's revisit the key strategies and tools you now have in your arsenal to navigate the digital world with confidence and care.

**Key Takeaways: Strategies for Digital Harmony**

The journey to digital wellness is paved with practical strategies and thoughtful action plans. Here's a recap of the essential tools we've explored:

- **Understanding Technology's Role**: Recognize both the benefits and risks of tech in your family's life. Celebrate its potential to connect, educate, and inspire while staying vigilant about its downsides, like overuse and dependency.
- **Creating a Healthy Balance**:
  - Set clear boundaries for screen time and device-free zones.
  - Use schedules and tools to encourage mindful tech use, like app timers or screen-free hours.

- **Digital Citizenship**: Teach kids to approach the online world with kindness, respect, and critical thinking. Encourage them to consider the long-term impact of their online actions and to prioritize positive interactions.
- **Recognizing Warning Signs**: Look out for symptoms of tech overuse, such as changes in mood, behavior, or sleep. Address these with calm, proactive measures, like setting family goals to reduce screen time.
- **Embracing Offline Activities**: Foster a love for non-digital hobbies, outdoor adventures, and quality face-to-face time to enrich family bonds and create lasting memories.

### Your Family Digital Wellness Plan

To make these strategies actionable, here's a simple, customizable template for creating your own family digital wellness plan.

#### Step 1: Define Goals

Start with one or two specific objectives:

- Example: Reduce daily screen time by 30 minutes.
- Example: Spend at least one tech-free evening together each week.

#### Step 2: Set Rules Together

Involve every family member to ensure buy-in:

- No phones at the dinner table.
- Devices go to a common charging station by 9 PM.

#### Step 3: Track Progress

Create a fun tracking system, like a family chart or stickers, to celebrate milestones.

**Step 4: Schedule Check-Ins**

Hold monthly family meetings to evaluate what's working and what needs adjusting.

**Step 5: Reward Efforts**

Acknowledge achievements with non-tech rewards, like a family outing or an extra bedtime story for younger kids.

**Empowering Parents for the Future**

As a parent in today's digital world, you're not just managing devices, you're shaping how your children approach technology for a lifetime. It's not always easy, but you're equipped with the wisdom and tools to guide them toward a balanced, healthy relationship with technology.

Remember, adaptability is your greatest asset. The digital landscape will keep evolving, with new apps, platforms, and trends always on the horizon. What remains constant is your ability to foster critical thinking, set thoughtful boundaries, and nurture meaningful connections with your children.

Every effort you make, whether it's a small conversation about online safety or a consistent family tech rule, plants seeds of lifelong wellness. You're not striving for perfection; you're aiming for progress.

**Next Steps: Small Changes, Lasting Impact**

The path to lifelong digital wellness begins today. Start with something manageable:

- Declare tonight a screen-free dinner.
- Try one of the activities from earlier chapters, like a family digital detox weekend.
- Talk with your kids about their favorite apps and what they enjoy about them, opening the door for meaningful dialogue.

Each step you take is a step closer to a future where technology supports your family's values instead of overshadowing them. Trust the process, celebrate the small wins, and remember: the effort you invest now will ripple across generations.

---

# Epilogue: A Legacy of Balance and Connection

The gentle hum of a phone vibrating on the counter was barely noticeable as Claire poured herself a cup of coffee. She glanced toward the living room, where her two kids were sprawled on the floor, working together on a puzzle they'd started over the weekend. No tablets, no TikTok, just laughter and the quiet hum of sibling teamwork. Claire smiled. It hadn't been easy getting here, but moments like this made it all worth it.

Technology is deeply woven into the fabric of our lives, shaping how we connect, learn, and even relax. Yet, as Claire discovered, it's not about rejecting it entirely. It's about finding a rhythm that lets tech enhance our lives without overshadowing the human experiences that truly matter.

### Reflecting on the Journey

Every family's relationship with technology is as unique as their story. Over the course of this book, we've explored the complexities of navigating a digital world: the highs of connection and creativity, the lows of overuse and dependency, and the subtle go-betweens where most of us live.

You've learned how to recognize warning signs of imbalance, set practical boundaries, and foster a culture of digital responsibility. Most importantly, you've discovered how to approach this ever-changing landscape with intention, creativity, and a sense of shared purpose.

### A New Chapter Awaits

The tools and strategies you've gathered are just the beginning. They are a foundation, but the real magic lies in how you'll adapt them to fit your family's evolving needs. There will be days when the balance feels effortless, and others when it's a struggle to keep everyone off their screens. That's okay. Progress isn't linear, and meaningful change takes time.

What matters most is your commitment to staying engaged. Whether it's starting a weekly tech-free tradition, discussing the latest viral trend with your teen, or simply being present during family meals, every small effort counts. These choices, repeated over time, will help create a legacy of thoughtful tech use that your kids can carry forward.

### Carrying the Torch

The digital age isn't going anywhere, but that's not something to fear. It's an opportunity, a chance to teach your children resilience, critical thinking, and empathy in ways that previous generations could only dream of. By guiding them to use technology as a tool, not a crutch, you're empowering them to navigate their future with confidence and grace.

Think of yourself not just as a gatekeeper of screen time, but as a mentor in digital citizenship. Your example, your patience, and your willingness to learn alongside your kids will leave an indelible mark on their relationship with technology, and, more importantly, with you.

### The Journey Forward

As you close this book, remember: the story of digital wellness doesn't have a neat ending. It's a living, breathing process, shaped by the choices you make every day. The conversations you start today will echo into the future, creating a ripple effect of awareness and connection.

So take a moment to pause. Reflect on how far you've come and what lies ahead. The journey isn't about perfection, it's about progress, curiosity, and the courage to keep trying. And in those moments of doubt or frustration, hold onto this truth: you're not just managing screens. You're nurturing a family that values connection, growth, and balance in a world that's always changing.

---

www.ingramcontent.com/pod-product-compliance
Lightning Source LLC
LaVergne TN
LVHW010606160826
845677LV00013B/3264

* 9 7 9 8 2 3 0 9 0 7 1 9 0 *